ADVANCED INTERVIEWING
TECHNIQUES

ABOUT THE AUTHORS

John R. Schafer, Ph.D. is a retired FBI Special Agent. He was assigned to the FBI's elite National Security Behavioral Analysis Program. Special Agent Schafer's investigative experience includes foreign counterintelligence, civil rights, crimes against children, and statement analyses. He also served as a pilot and a Korean linguist early in his FBI career. Special Agent Schafer earned a Bachelor of Arts degree in psychology from Western Illinois University, a Bachelor of Arts degree in business administration from Elmhurst College, and a Master of Arts degree in criminal justice from Western Illinois University. He earned a Ph.D. in psychology from Fielding Graduate University. Dr. Schafer has published numerous articles in magazines and professional journals.

Joe Navarro, received his undergraduate degree from Brigham Young University and his Master of Arts degree in International Relations from Salve Regina University. He retired from the FBI after 25 years of dedicated service to his country having served both as a Special Agent and as a Supervisor. He served in the Phoenix, New York, San Juan, and Tampa Divisions of the FBI handling complex counterintelligence and counterterrorism, investigations. For most of his Bureau career, Mr. Navarro was also an educator teaching a variety of topics to both the law enforcement and intelligence community. He was a founding member of the FBI's elite National Security Division–Behavioral Analysis Program where he served as an expert in interviewing and nonverbal behavior. He continues to teach for the

FBI as well as other members of the intelligence community and is on the adjunct faculty at the University of Tampa, the National College of District Attorneys, and Saint Leo's University in Florida. Mr. Navarro travels throughout the world sharing his unique knowledge and experiences in the area of interviewing and nonverbal communications with law enforcement, military, security, and intelligence professionals.

Second Edition

ADVANCED INTERVIEWING TECHNIQUES

Proven Strategies for Law Enforcement, Military, and Security Personnel

By

JOHN R. SCHAFER, PH.D.

FBI Special Agent (Ret.)
National Security Division
Behavior Analysis Program

and

JOE NAVARRO, M.A.

FBI Special Agent (Ret.)
National Security Division
Behavioral Analysis Program

CHARLES C THOMAS · PUBLISHER, LTD.
Springfield · Illinois · U.S.A.

Published and Distributed Throughout the World by

CHARLES C THOMAS • PUBLISHER, LTD.
2600 South First Street
Springfield, Illinois 62704

©2010 by CHARLES C THOMAS • PUBLISHER, LTD.

ISBN 978-0-398-07942-0 (hard)
ISBN 978-0-398-07943-7 (paper)

Library of Congress Catalog Card Number: 2010008557

Printed in the United States of America
TS-R-3

Library of Congress Cataloging-in-Publication Data

Schafer, John R., 1954–
    Advanced interviewing techniques : proven strategies for law enforcement, military
and security personnel / by John R. Schafer and Joe Navarro. -- 2nd ed.
        p. cm.
    Includes bibliographical references and index.
    ISBN 978-0-398-07942-0 (hard) -- ISBN 978-0-398-07943-7 (pbk)
    1. Police questinging 2. Military interrogation. I. Navarro, Joe, 1953– II. Title.

HV8073.S27 2010
363.25′4--dc22

                                                                                2010008557

PREFACE

The purpose of this book is to update the previous edition with the latest interviewing techniques. New techniques and discoveries in psychology and related fields require interviewers keep current with the latest interview and interrogation techniques.

As with the previous book, this edition was written with working professionals in mind and contains advanced interviewing techniques. Some basic topics emphasized in other interviewing books will not be addressed. This book was designed as a quick reference guide rather than a comprehensive manual. The enhanced outline format of the text and the extended table of contents provide for easy reference, reading, and comprehension.

Material for this book derived from numerous sources including formal interviewing models and decades of social and psychological research as well as the authors' over fifty years of combined law enforcement experience. In many instances, this book provides names for techniques instinctively used by experienced investigators. Identifying and explaining interviewing techniques afford investigators with less experience the opportunity to use the same effective techniques as do their more experienced colleagues.

The marketplace is replete with interviewing books and manuals; however, quickly locating information buried in thick manuscripts is costly and time consuming. The style of this book is consistent with the manner in which law enforcement officers like to receive information: quickly, authoritatively, and to the point.

INTRODUCTION

Traditionally, obtaining information from others is divided into two categories, the interview and the interrogation. The interview, a more benign inquiry, gleans facts from witnesses and other people not directly related to the activity under investigation. The interrogation, a more intimidating process, extracts information from unwilling suspects. This two-paradigm approach suggests that the mindset of the investigator during an interview differs from the mindset of the investigator during an interrogation. Consequently, investigators adopt one persona during an interview and a more aggressive persona during an interrogation. Changing from the interview persona to the interrogation persona can be difficult, especially when interviewing witnesses who, for various reasons, offer resistance similar to suspects.

An alternative approach to the inquiry process places the interview on a resistance continuum. At one end of the continuum, interviewees offer information without resistance. At the other end, interviewees are reluctant to provide information or fall silent. This concept allows investigators to glide back and forth along the resistance continuum using a succession of specialized interviewing techniques to overcome varying degrees of resistance. Investigators need only focus on the appropriate selection of interviewing techniques to overcome resistance from witnesses and suspects alike. As the interviewee's resistance increases or decreases, the interviewer adjusts the intensity of the inquiry by selecting the suitable interviewing technique to overcome the interviewee's resistance.

Merely learning a variety of interviewing techniques, however, does not make a good interviewer. A good interviewer not only knows how to use interviewing techniques but can also identify the appropriate circumstances in which to use each technique. Using an interviewing technique at the wrong time can have a negative impact on the outcome of an interview. Investigators must exercise appropriate caution when using any advanced interviewing techniques.

Good interviewers glean techniques from formal training, personal experience, and fellow investigators, and then assimilate those techniques into their own personalities. When interviewing techniques become part of an investigator's personality, the investigator can act naturally during an interview without the added pressure of maintaining a pretense.

No single interviewing method or technique provides a magic formula for success. The fact remains, investigators only become good interviewers by interviewing. Every interview, no matter how trivial, provides an opportunity to practice new interviewing techniques or to hone previously learned skills.

An interviewing technique that works for one investigator might not work for another investigator, and, of course, each interviewee is different. If a particular interviewing technique does not work the first time, the investigator should change one or more aspects of the technique or add a personal touch. If the technique still does not work, discard it no matter how effective other investigators judge the technique.

Whether investigators subscribe to the traditional interview/interrogation approach or to the resistance continuum, effective communication with a purpose remains at the core of the interviewing process. This book builds on interviewers' communication skills and expands their repertoire of interviewing techniques.

The first three chapters examine interview planning, the interview setting, and the use of interview props, the foundation for effective inquiry. The next four chapters, assessing the interviewee, establishing dominance, building rapport, and Miranda warnings focus on establishing effective communications under legal constraints. Chapters 8, 9, and 10 discuss deception and the verbal and nonverbal cues to detecting deception. Chapter 11 provides investigators with a variety of interviewing tools to overcome interviewee resistance. Chapter 12 demonstrates techniques to deal with angry people. Chapter 13 reviews techniques to break the interview impasse, a critical point in the inquiry. The final chapter focuses on the interview end game, an often overlooked component of the interview process.

CONTENTS

ADVANCED INTERVIEWING TECHNIQUES

Planning the Interview

Planning is the most important aspect in the interview process; yet, it is the most overlooked. Interviewers typically do not plan for interviews because they are either too busy or, for various reasons, do not feel the need to plan. Interview preparation is neither difficult nor time-consuming once interviewers develop a mental checklist applicable to most routine interviews. Of course, more complex interviews require more in-depth thought and planning.

Selecting the Interviewer

Interviewers should read the case file, learn about the suspect, and then ask themselves two questions, "If I were the suspect, who would I want to interview me and why?" and "Am I the best person to do this interview?" If the investigation is important and you know you are not the right person to do the interview, select a more suitable interviewer. Be honest with yourself.

If two interviewers conduct an interview, both interviewers should plan to take the primary role in the event the initial interviewer and the interviewee experience a personality clash.

Number of Interviewers

One-on-one interviews create an environment with the highest probability of success. If a one-on-one interview is not possible, no more than two interviewers should conduct the interview. More than two interviewers raise the anxiety level of the interviewee and could inhibit the rapport-building process between the interviewee and the interviewer.

Multiple interviewers may be perceived as an audience giving the interviewee an opportunity to put on a performance to advance his or her personal or social agenda instead of answering questions. In some situations, the presence of multiple interviewers promote competition between the interviewers, which is nonproductive and detracts from the focus of the interview (Meloy & Mohandie, 2002).

Age of the Interviewer

The age of the interviewer should be considered. An older interviewer may provide a substitute father figure for an interviewee who was abandoned by his or her father during childhood. Fatherly or authoritarian feelings can be exploited during the interview (Meloy & Mohandie, 2002). An interviewer who is younger than the interviewee may be perceived by the interviewee as a person who can be manipulated due to inexperience or naiveté. A younger interviewer could also assume the role of a student or apprentice for an interviewee who views himself or herself as a teacher or mentor.

Gender of the Interviewer(s)

In most instances, the gender of the interviewer will not affect the outcome of the interview. However, under certain conditions, the gender of the interviewer may have a positive or negative impact on the interview. A female interviewer interviewing a male suspect may evoke emotions from the suspect that can be exploited depending on the personality and culture of the interviewee and the interview objectives. A female interviewer interviewing a Middle Eastern suspect may prove more difficult because Middle Eastern males often view women as having more traditional or domesticated roles (Nydell, 1996).

Interview Objectives

Take time before the interview to think. Establish clear, attainable objectives. Carefully define your objectives. Well-defined goals increase the probability of success because the interview will proceed with direction and purpose.

Confession

If the goal of the interview is a confession, review the appropriate statutes and memorize the legal elements necessary to prove the crime. A confession is less effective if the suspect does not confess to all the elements necessary to prove the criminal violation in a courtroom. Keep in mind that some suspects will not formally confess, but rather make a series of smaller admissions, which in concert constitute a full confession.

Lead Information

If the objective of the interview is to obtain information of lead value, identify the specific information needed and either solicit the information using a straightforward approach or develop strategies to elicit the information using more subtle techniques.

Informant Development

If the goal of the interview is to develop an informant, establishing rapport, the foundation for a long-term relationship, is the paramount objective. A slower, more measured approach is typically more effective in building a lasting relationship based on trust.

Gathering Intelligence

If the goal of the interview is to gather intelligence, then any information from the interviewee may be significant. The interviewer should keep the interviewee talking for as long as possible. The primary goal of an intelligence interview is to obtain as much information as possible. Interviewers should not restrict themselves to the elements of the crime but widen the scope of the interview to as many relevant topics as possible.

The Importance of Confessions

At trial, the mere presentation of a confession increases the rate of guilty verdicts. Confession evidence is more powerful than eyewitness identifications and character witnesses. In fact, "Confession evidence is so inherently prejudicial that people do not fully discount the information even when it is logically and legally appropriate to do so" (Kassin, 1997).

The Interview as Theater

Everything and everybody on the interview stage should serve one purpose: Move the inquiry toward the interview objectives. As with any stage production, the dialog, the props, the costumes, and the actors have specific functions and the interviewer acts as the director in the unfolding drama.

The interviewer plans the location (the stage) and the time of day for the interview, writes the interview script, chooses the actors, and selects the props in a coordinated effort to achieve the interview objectives.

Scripting an interview is important. Some of the best interviewers script their interviews and memorize as much information about the case as practical. Words are the interviewer's primary tool. The great philosopher Carl Wittgenstein stated, "The limits of my language mean the limits of my world." Investigators must know and understand the appropriate street slang or technical terms prior to beginning an interview. Learning jargon is especially important in computer fraud, white-collar, and denial of service investigations.

Rehearsals are important for the success of any stage performance, and so it is with interviews. Rehearse the introduction, seating arrangements, and any other contingencies such as the presence of a friend, attorney, or parent. Use all your senses. Feel the atmosphere in the interview room. Sense the tension level of the upcoming interview.

Role Playing

Just prior to the interview or driving to meet the interviewee, interviewers should role-play the interview: one investigator takes the part of the interviewee and the other interviewer takes the part of the interviewer. Each interviewer then challenges the other with scenarios that are likely to be played out during the interview. Role-playing mentally prepares the interviewers long before the interview actually begins.

Visualize yourself interacting with the interviewee. Listen to yourself as you mentally play out interview strategies in your mind. The more you plan and rehearse, the greater the chances are that you will succeed. Nothing guarantees a successful interview, but lack of proper planning opens the door to failure.

Calling an Audible

No matter how much you plan and rehearse the interview, things will go wrong. If the preplanned strategy fails, interviewers should be prepared to instantly change the scope, direction, and interview techniques. Flexibility provides the interviewer with an opportunity to use additional tools to achieve the interview objectives.

Time of Day to Conduct an Interview

Determining the optimal time of day to conduct an interview is based on an assessment of the interviewee and the scope and intensity of the interview topics. Will the interview objectives be best achieved when the interviewee is tired and worn down or fresh and robust?

Morning
Typically, people are alert during the morning hours and are more attentive to details. Morning interviews provide the interviewer with sufficient time to conduct in-depth inquiries.

Afternoon
Late afternoon interviews produce the most confessions because people are physically and mentally fatigued. Afternoon interviews can be problematic in that the interviewee may have to pick up children from daycare or school. In larger cities, heavy rush-hour traffic may place an artificial time limit on the interview. If the interview is conducted in the interviewee's workspace, overtime payment may limit the length of the interview. Many interviews prematurely end because the interviewee wants to go home on time.

Evening
Most people are physically and mentally fatigued at the end of the day. Depending on the nature of the inquiry and the interview objectives, an evening interview at the interviewer's residence may be

appropriate. One advantage of an evening interview is that the suspect may be more cooperative without the presence of peers, coworkers, or coconspirators.

The Interview Venue

The interview location sends a message to the interviewee. Interviewers should wisely choose an interview setting that is consistent with the interview objectives and a location that enables the interviewer to control time, space, and the environment as much as practical.

Police Station

A police station presents an intimidating environment, clearly placing the interviewer in complete control of the interview theater. However, a police station may not be the best place to conduct interviews because the intimidating setting may inhibit interviewees from speaking openly and honestly.

Interviewee's Workspace

An interview conducted in the interviewee's workspace puts the interviewer at a disadvantage in that the interviewee controls the interview theater. The interviewee usually feels secure and comfortable in his or her personal environment. On the other hand, the interviewee will inevitably be the focus of attention when the investigator arrives and departs. The demeanor of the interviewer when he or she enters and exits the interviewee's workspace can enhance or diminish the reaction of the interviewee's supervisor and coworkers. In many instances, discretion provides an incentive for the interviewee to cooperate.

Interviewee's Residence

An interviewee feels most secure in his or her own residence because he or she has complete control of the interview theater. The interviewer is a guest and can be asked to leave at any time. An advantage to interviewing a suspect or witnesses at his or her residence is that the interviewer has the opportunity to survey and evaluate the contents of the interviewee's home. With a multiple interview strategy, the interviewer gains valuable insight into the interviewee's personality and lifestyle. Another advantage of an in-residence interview is that the suspect is more likely to allow a consent search of his or her home or computer.

Automobile

Cars are poor interview settings because the interviewer and the interviewee are either sitting side by side in the front seat or the interviewer must turn to talk to the suspect who is sitting in the rear seat. The closed environment severely limits the range of techniques available to the interviewer. Automobiles are best suited to debrief informants since the relationship between the interviewer and an informant is usually more cordial and less adversarial.

Restaurant

Restaurants and other public places are neutral areas where interviewers can meet interviewees and still maintain limited control of the interview theater. In multiple interview strategies, a restaurant is an ideal place for the first meeting. If the interview is being recorded, interviewers should visit the restaurant prior to the interview at the same time the interview is scheduled. During non-peak hours the restaurant background noise may be acceptable for recording, however, during peak times, the increased background noise may produce poor quality recordings.

Videotaping Interviews

A visible camera may have a chilling effect on the interviewee. However, several minutes into the interview, the interviewee tends to forget the presence of a discretely installed video camera. Your agency's policy and state and federal laws should govern the use of video cameras during interviews.

Videotaping an interview makes it possible for one interviewer to conduct the interview because any statements made by the suspect are recorded. Videotaping an interview also relieves the interviewer of the burden of taking notes and allows the interviewer to concentrate all his or her energies on conducting the interview.

The camera angle is a very important consideration. When videotaping an interview, only the suspect should be framed. Focusing solely on the suspect decreases the impact of the interviewer's actions on the jury (Lassiter, Shaw, Briggs, & Scanlan, 1992). Keep in mind that you must live with whatever is on the videotape.

Notepads

In suspect interviews, avoid using yellow legal notepads because they may have an adverse effect as legal pads symbolize lawyers and courtrooms (Inbau, Reid, Buckley, & Jayne, 1986). If note taking is required, the investigator should use 3 x 5 inch note cards or similar nondescript paper.

Note Taking

An alternate method to traditional note taking is to allow the interviewee to take notes for you. Pass a notepad to the interviewee and tell him or her to write down specific information because you want to ensure addresses are accurate, names are spelled correctly, and information is recorded correctly. During the interview summary, tell the interviewee that to ensure accuracy, it is better that he or she should write down a summary of the interview because you don't want to take a chance misinterpreting anything the interviewee said. Instruct the interviewee to initial each page and sign and date the last page to eliminate the possibility that someone could alter the notes. This note-taking technique takes practice. Interviewers should practice this technique during witness interviews because any mistakes made during witness interviews can be easily corrected. With a little practice, interviewers should be able to conduct suspect interviews using this method. Note taking using this technique is equivalent to a signed statement.

Note Taking

Interviewers memorialize important facts. They do not write down trivia or record information that they already know and therefore, should avoid taking notes only when interviewees make incriminating statements. The interviewer's note-taking patterns enable the intervie-wee to evaluate how much information the interviewer really knows about the investigation, which may negate a bluff later in the interview or cause the suspect to obfuscate certain topics raised during the inter-view.

The Learning Curve

Acquiring new skills requires practice. During the practice period, people sometimes become discouraged and give up for various reasons including embarrassment, lack of immediate mastery of the new skills, or frustration.

The Learning Curve illustrates how people acquire new skills. The first step in the learning process is the Free Fall. During this time, people are not comfortable using the new skills and become frus-trated or embarrassed when the skills do not work as intended. Instead of continuing to practice the skills, people often quit prac-ticing them and revert back to using the less effective skills they are more comfortable using. Learners must persevere through the Free Fall until they achieve Skill Mastery. The frustration and dis-comfort of acquiring new skills is well worth the effort because the learner's new skill level will be far greater than the learner's initial skill level. Investigators should practice the interviewing tech-niques outlined in this book until they achieve Skill Mastery. Mas-tering interviewing techniques increase the likelihood of conducting successful interviews and increase the interviewer's ability to detect deception and obtain the truth.

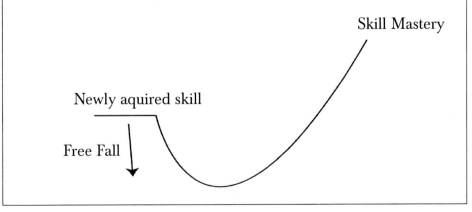

The Interview

Setting

Everything and every person in the interview theater serves a purpose. The type of interview setting depends on the interview objectives, the person being interviewed, and the specific circumstances surrounding the inquiry. Careful preparation of the interview setting gives interviewers a psychological edge. It is crucial that the interviewers control and dominate the interview setting no matter how adverse the conditions.

Physical Space

A quiet place with few distractions provides the optimum interview setting (Inbau, 1999; Inbau et al., 1986; Vessel, 1998; Szczesny, 2002). Cell phones should be turned off during the interview or not permitted in the interview setting. Interviewees who are under pressure often seek out distractions such as cell phones to avoid answering difficult questions.

Obstacles

Obstacles such as tables or desks should not block a head-to-toe view of the interviewee's body (Inbau et al., 1986). Obscuring the interviewee's lower body deprives the interviewer of vital nonverbal behaviors such as fidgeting, shuffling, or foot positioning (Lewis, 1995; Navarro & Schafer, 2001). If a head-to-toe observation is not possible, interviewers should position themselves to observe as much of the body as possible.

In an uncontrolled environment where the interviewer does not control furniture placement, the interviewer should sit near the corner of the table or desk angled toward the interviewee. This position provides an unobstructed view of the interviewee and neutralizes the interviewee's use of the table or desk as a blocking device.

Chair Placement within a Room

The interviewee's chair should be placed as close to the door as practical. Psychologically, there is less stress near a door because the door represents a physical and psychological escape. Another strategy is to place the interviewer's chair between the suspect and the door. This placement sends a message to the interviewee that he must go through the interviewer to gain his or her freedom. The interviewer could also place the interviewee's chair up against the wall. Like the chair, the interviewee will feel as through his or her back is against the wall.

Door Jamb Admissions

Interviewees will sometimes make admissions as they leave the interview room. The door represents a physical and psychological escape and interviewees often feel compelled to "throw a bone" to the interviewers as they approach the door (Navarro, 2000).

Individual Chair Placement

Males

When interviewing males, position the interviewer's chair at an angle to the interviewee's chair (Lewis, 1995; Wainwright, 1993). Face-to-face seating is confrontational and inhibits rapport development (Lewis, 1995; Wainwright, 1993). If a face-to-face interview cannot be avoided, the interviewer should, at least, sit askance. As the interview develops, the interviewer could gradually maneuver his or her chair to a more adversarial position.

Females

When interviewing females, place the interviewer's chair directly across from interviewee's chair (Lewis, 1995). Females are more comfortable conversing face-to-face (Wainwright, 1993). Later, during the interview, the interviewer could adjust his or her chair as required.

Seating Arrangements

People in cooperative relationships sit side-by-side (Wainwright, 1993). If the interviewer's chair has wheels or easily slides, the interviewer could, at the appropriate moment, roll or slide his or her chair alongside the interviewee to encourage cooperation. Wheeled chairs also allow the interviewer to move closer to or farther away from the interviewer, thus increasing or decreasing the tension of the interview (Inbau et al., 1986).

Chair Placement for a Second Interviewer

Interviewers should set the chair for the second interviewer at an angle to the interviewee's chair and slightly behind the interviewer's chair. This position encourages the interviewee to develop rapport with the primary interviewer. If the second interviewer takes notes, set his or her chair in the area of the interviewee's peripheral vision. This position reduces the possibility that the interviewee will monitor note-taking patterns.

Chair Placement for a Third Party

Set the chair for a parent or an attorney at an angle to the interviewee's chair but slightly farther back in the area of the interviewee's peripheral vision. The third party may adjust his or her chair; nevertheless, chair placement sends a subtle message that his or her participation in the interview is peripheral.

Props

Props reaffirm the interviewer's verbal and nonverbal messages. Props also send silent messages for the interviewee to interpret within the context of his or her guilty knowledge; however, not all interviews require props. Perception plays a significant role in obtaining confessions. The stronger the evidence, real or perceived, the more likely the interviewee will confess (Kassin, 1997; Cassell & Hayman, 1996; Canter & Alison, 1999; White, 2001). Props bolster the illusion that the interviewer possesses strong evidence. Plan the use of props well in advance of the interview and carefully decide the purpose of each prop and anticipate the effect on the interviewee. Each interview scenario requires specially designed props that meet the interview objectives; nonetheless, universal props do exist. Props can be very effective interviewing tools if used properly; however, an improperly used prop can cause serious credibility problems for the interviewer.

Certificates and Awards

A wall covered with photos, awards, and certificates lends credibility and authority to the interviewer (Pease, 1984). However, people who display certificates, awards, and pictures of themselves with celebrities are sometimes viewed as insecure (Lewis, 1995) and appear self-centered and arrogant (Dimitrius & Mazzarella, 2000). As with all props, certificates, awards, and pictures should further specific interview objectives.

File Cabinets

File cabinets in the interview room with labels bearing the interviewee's name in bold letters or labels marked "Evidence recovered at (name of the coconspirator)'s residence" gives the illusion that the interviewer(s) know more about the investigation than they really do.

Documents

Barely visible documents strategically placed in the interviewer's notebook titled "Statement of (insert the name of the interviewee's coconspirator)" or "Immunity Agreement of (insert the name of the interviewee's coconspirator)" can be very persuasive. When the interviewer opens his or her notebook, the suspect will see the barely visible document(s) and think that he or she now possesses privileged information.

If the interviewee resists telling the truth, the interviewer might tell the interviewee that his or her coconspirator(s) cooperated with the investigation and that the interviewer knows the whole story. Not revealing the existence of the documents forces the suspect to speculate as to how much evidence the investigator possesses. Nagging doubts coupled with guilty knowledge enhance the probability that the bluff will succeed.

Case Files

The interviewer could carry a thick manila folder with the suspect's name clearly visible on the file tab. The thick file suggests to the suspect that the interviewer amassed a great deal of information regarding the suspect and the investigation. The size of the fake case files should be proportionate with the crime committed. Bringing a large case file to an interview of a petty thief damages the interviewer's credibility.

Security Camera

The interviewer could bring a videocassette wrapped in evidence tape with words, "Security camera from (a business located at or near the scene of the crime) (date of the crime)" written on the label. The videocassette suggests to the interviewee that a security camera recorded the crime. If the suspect asks to view the tape, tell him or her that the tape was just recovered and will be sent to the laboratory for processing. This prop can be used in a variety of bluffs.

Investigator: "What do you think I'll see on the tape?" The suspect's initial response may reveal his or her mindset.

Investigator: "If you're lying now and the tape shows that you were there, it's a whole new ballgame. Do you want to gamble that you're not on the tape?"

Another investigator interrupts the interview and request to speak with the interviewer. After several minutes, the interviewer returns with the video tape and tells the suspect, "Now's the time to talk before I play the video. Things will only get worse for you from now on."

Photographs

Photographs of the crime scene or of the victim(s) are often helpful in getting suspects to react. Sometimes suspects respond contritely and make admissions, or indicate that they will tell the truth if the photos are taken away because they do not want to relive the horror of their crime.

The investigator places a picture of two people who the investigator identifies as the victim's mother and father in front of the suspect and asks, "If you could talk to them now, what would you tell them?" The suspect's answer can reveal hints as to the suspect's guilt or innocence.

Putting the Puzzle Together

When sending a message to a suspect, the interviewer should subtly present clues. Let the suspects put the clues together. When people put the pieces of the puzzle together themselves, the message becomes credible because they thought of it themselves rather than being told what to think by the interviewer, whose believability and motives are suspect. Additionally, suspects attach meaning to the message within the context of their personal circumstances and/or guilty knowledge. The most common mistake made by investigators is "shouting" their message because they believe the suspect will not understand otherwise. This is not the case. Suspects are keenly aware of every nuance of the interview including the interviewer's verbal and nonverbal behaviors. A suspect may not be formally educated, but reading people is essential for his or her survival on the streets.

A Coconspirator

Use a coconspirator as a prop by having him or her be seen by the suspect prior to entering the interview room. Just the presence of a coconspirator may force the suspect to reconsider a decision not to cooperate with the investigator because the suspect will always wonder if the coconspirator will cooperate in exchange for a plea bargaining advantage. Whether or not the coconspirator cooperates, his or her mere presence lends credibility to any bluffs presented during the interview.

Telephone Call

The telephone is a dynamic prop. A strategic telephone call from an unseen investigator may serve to put the interviewee on notice of newfound evidence or that a coconspirator made critical admissions. The interviewer can send a powerful message to the suspect by allowing him or her to overhear at least one side of a cryptic telephone conversation.

Signed Statements Almost

If interviewing uncooperative coconspirators separately, get one to write "I have told the investigators the whole truth," and have him or her sign it. Once signed, walk in on the other suspect and ask what he or she has to say after showing him or her the signed statement. Many times the interviewee will cooperate, and curse the coconspirators (Navarro, 2000).

Assessing the Interviewee

Interviewers may have several months or several minutes to assess suspects or witnesses. The key to assessing interviewees is to evaluate their general attributes, clusters of behaviors, clothes, and accessories. Identifying specific personality traits and disorders provides interviewers with detailed information to structure a formal interview. If time does not permit an in-depth assessment of suspects or witnesses, interviewers should assess interviewees during the first few minutes of the interview or, if possible, watch suspects or witnesses as they approach the interviewing venue. The manner in which interviewees approach the interview venue could reveal their true emotional state. Are they taking deep breaths to prepare for the confrontation ahead? Are they hesitant and nervous? or are they comfortable and relaxed?

Social Indices

Clothing

Clothing is a key indicator of social status (Molloy, 1975; Dimitrius & Mazzarella, 2000). A person who wears a suit and tie is in a different state of mind from a person who wears blue jeans and a T-shirt, or a person who wears slacks and a polo shirt. Generally, an interviewer can determine the social status of the interviewee and thereby anticipate certain attitudes and behaviors. Cars, tattoos, bumper stickers, and other social artifacts are good social and political indicators (Navarro & Schafer, 2003).

Appearance

People with "baby faces" are perceived as warm, honest, trustworthy, submissive, naive, and relatively incompetent. Conversely, mature individuals are perceived as strong leaders, dominant, aggressive, and competent. Attractive people are seen as having more positive attributes than less attractive people (Feingold, 1992; Berry & Landry, 1997; Dimitrius & Mazzarella, 2000). Attractive people are also less likely to be convicted in a jury trial and if convicted, receive less severe sentences (Michelini & Sodgrass, 1980; Efran, 1974, Steward, 1980).

Briefcase

People who do all the work carry large, bulky briefcases. People with authority carry slim briefcases.

Office Space

Higher status people have the largest offices with the best views. Space is a symbol of power and status (Lewis, 1995). Large offices with wasted space indicate the occupant has high status. Only high-status people can afford to waste office or residential space.

A clean, well-organized office suggests that the occupant is conscientious and agreeable (Gosling, Ko, Mannarelli, & Morris, 2002). Additionally, the occupant of an office with distinctive décor and a variety (not quantity) of magazines and CDs on display is judged as open-minded (Gosling et al., 2002).

Office Location

The closer a person's office is to the office occupied by final decision-makers in an organization, the more power and status the person possesses (Lewis, 1995).

Pay Attention to Details

People who try to portray themselves as having more status than they actually possess will wear the right clothes but will often forget about the accessories (Lewis, 1995). A man may dress in a power suit and tie but fail to polish his shoes or carry a well-worn wallet. This lack of attention to detail might suggest the person is feigning social status.

Spot and Assess*

The Spot and Assess technique quickly and efficiently gleans large amounts of information. The interviewer begins with the interviewee and addresses the following topics, people, places, equipment, and money. The interviewee begins with the interviewee and describes him or her using the Top Down/Outside In method. The interviewer begins with the interviewee's hair and moves downward to the interviewee's feet describing the interviewee's, scars, marks, and tattoos. The interviewee then starts from the outside and moves inward describing the interviewee's style of clothing and accessories such as watches and jewelry. The Top Down/Outside In method can also be used to describe inanimate objects such as vehicles and houses. Interviewees take up space so the interviewer should describe the place where the interviewee is or references in his or her responses. If the interviewee reports that he began his day at his house, the interviewer should get a description of the interviewee's house using the Top Down/Outside In method. People need equipment to get from one place to another place or to accomplish tasks. The interviewer should get a description of equipment used by the interviewee. Equipment includes vehicles, weapons, or any other items used to accomplish tasks. Money is required to live and to buy equipment. The interviewer should ask the interviewee for the source of money that allows him or her to live and buy equipment. The interviewer now has enough information to assess the interviewee for the relevance and veracity of the information provided by the interviewee. Each time the interviewee introduces another person or moves to another location, the interviewer should repeat the Spot and Assess technique.

---

* The Spot and Assess technique was initially developed by George Akkelquest and modified by the author.

Desk Configurations

A desk positioned diagonally across the office space, or a desk facing the door, or a desk that disproportionately divides the room indicates low to moderate status (Lewis, 1995). A desk positioned against a wall signals moderate to high status. High status is portrayed when the occupant of the desk can look out the window and his or her back faces the door (Lewis, 1995).

Residential Space[1]

A clean, well-organized home suggests the resident is conscientious and agreeable (Gosling et al., 2002). On the other hand, a person with a cluttered house with clothes strewn about is seen as disorganized and not very conscientious. Homes that have distinctive décors and display a variety of books, magazines, and CDs suggest to the observer that the occupants are open-minded (Gosling et al., 2002).

Physical Stature

Posture and stride might indicate the mental state of the interviewee (Nierenberg & Calero, 1971). Shoulders hunched and a slow gait signal lack of enthusiasm and reticence to be interviewed. Shoulders back and a quick gait indicate that the interviewee is confident and expresses a willingness to be interviewed.

Age

Children

Investigators often overlook children as witnesses. Children can provide vital information especially in domestic violence investigations (Ennis, 2000). Notwithstanding, children may inaccurately perceive their world and may mistake what they remember if not questioned properly. The very young often engage in magical thinking (Chandler & Afifi, 1996). Assess child interviewees carefully, especially when sexual allegations are made. Children are easily misled by the type of questions interviewers ask. Interviewers should avoid leading questions when interviewing children (Bruck, 1999).

---

[1] The findings of Gosling, Ko, Mannarelli, and Morris (2002) are restricted to bedrooms; however, generalizing the findings to the entire residence is logical in that people live in entire houses and not just their bedrooms.

Teenagers

Teenagers may seem aloof and disrespectful and may seek to denigrate the interviewer because they perceive themselves as having special knowledge and a sense of invincibility.

Elderly

The elderly may find that their perceptions and recall are not what they use to be and should be vetted early in the interview to determine the accuracy of statements. Dementia and mental health may also be factors to consider. Simple questions about the interviewee's recent and distant memories can discreetly determine mental acuity.

Culture and Ethnicity

The culture and ethnicity of the interviewee are important considerations. Significant problems may arise if the interviewer is from one cultural group and the interviewee belongs to another. The successful investigator must first understand ethnic customs and cultural traditions and then determine if a specific behavioral pattern is appropriate within that particular cultural context. Several examples of cultural differences are cited below. Interviewers should keep in mind cultural patterns are generalizations that can change over time, acculturation, and from one person to the next.

American Indians

Many American Indians believe that humans must act in harmony with nature to achieve a spiritual understanding of life. Harmony between man and nature can be achieved through a variety of religious and traditional ceremonies usually performed by a medicine man (Schafer & McIlwaine, 1992). However, each Indian tribe has its own unique customs and beliefs. Socially correct behavior in one tribal setting may not be acceptable behavior in a different tribal setting.

American Indians often measure time in terms of day or night, by seasons, or by tribal events or religious ceremonies (Schafer & McIlwaine, 1992). Knowledge of special tribal ceremonies or religious events is a useful method to narrow the time frame within which the crime occurred or to better understand the mindset of the victim, witness, or suspect (Schafer & McIlwaine, 1992).

Cross-cultural Lie Detection

People from different cultures display similar deceptive behavioral cues. In fact, people from one culture judge the veracity of people from another culture more accurately than those from their own cultures (Al-Simadi, 2000).

Arabs and Muslims

Arabs prefer to discuss general personal or family health concerns at the beginning of the interview. Ask the Arab interviewee about his health and the health of his family. However, do not make specific inquiries regarding the interviewee's wife because traditional Arab males tend to protect Arab women from outsiders (Navarro, 2002).

Beyond the obvious language problems, there are cultural considerations when interviewing Arabs. Use cultural differences as a starting point to begin building rapport by asking about the interviewee's experiences in his or her own country and in this country. Talking about the interviewee's home country and how he or she immigrated to the United States is a good conversation starter. Another conversation starter is sports, especially soccer. Be courteous and respectful; many Arabs come from oppressive regimes and may equate American law enforcement officers to their own country's repressive internal security forces (Navarro, 2002).

Arabs tend not to reveal their true feelings, but rather behave in a manner consistent with social expectations (Al-Simadi, 2000). In the Arab culture, exposing the soles of one's shoes to another person is considered an insult (Nydell, 1996).

Arabs are visual thinkers. They think in pictures. Interviewers should paint pictures when describing concepts to Arab interviewees. Instead of asking Arab interviewees, "Please describe that person for me" interviewers should ask specific questions, "What color hair?;" What color eyes?"; "Was his beard short?"; "What color was his beard?"; etc.

Associative Thinking

Arabs are associative thinkers. They develop conversations topically. Conversations with Arabs often take a circuitous route before arriving at the answer to a specific question. Conversely, Westerners generally relate facts chronologically. Converting associative thinking to chronological thinking helps interviewers identify intelligence gaps and allow Arab thinkers to respond in a manner that is most familiar to them. To convert associative thinking to chronological thinking the investigator should allow the Arab speaker to complete topical answers. The interviewer then places the topical answers on a timeline. Placement on the timeline reveals chronological information gaps. The interviewer then asks specific questions that close the gaps in the time-line.

African-Americans

Typically, African-Americans are taught to look down or away from parental authority as a form of respect. When interviewing African-Americans, investigators should bear in mind that the lack of eye contact is not always an indicator of deception. Eye avoidance behavior is more typical of older African-Americans. Younger African-Americans are being reared in a different cultural environment and may not display eye avoidance behavior in the presence of authority figures.

Perception is important in multicultural settings. Caucasians elbowing one another is seen as a jovial gesture; however, African-Americans consider this same gesture as a sign of aggression (Kunda & Thagard, 1996; Duncan, 1976; Sagar & Schofield, 1980).

Drug-dependent Persons

A drug addict's loyalty is often dependent on the nature of their addiction. Typically, addicts are only loyal to their habit and to those who supply them with illicit drugs. The drug addict's chief concern is that cooperating with the police may jeopardize his or her drug supply.

Personality Disorders and Mental Illness

Personality traits are more or less permanent and seldom change throughout a person's life (APA, 1994). Personality disorders occur when personality traits become immutable to the point of causing personal and social impairment (APA, 1994). Investigators should not rely on one personality trait but, rather, clusters of traits to norm behavior.

The Narcissist

The narcissist is preoccupied with grandiosity and self-importance (APA, 1994). Narcissists crave admiration and feel that they are unique individuals and superior to others (APA, 1994). Narcissists believe that they are entitled to abundant admiration and the best amenities the world has to offer. Narcissists present an arrogant, haughty, or patronizing demeanor (APA, 1994). Narcissists have little regard for others and often wittingly or unwittingly exploit others (APA, 1994). Narcissists only enter into personal relationships with people who can enhance their self-esteem. Narcissists often feel they can handle any situation and are less likely to ask for legal assistance.

Investigators should avoid criticizing narcissists because they are very sensitive to attacks on their self-esteem.

Narcissists gradually come to grips with reality, especially when they are confronted with facts and files replete with incriminating information.

Investigators should take advantage of the narcissist's sense of entitlement. "Because of your superior talents, of course, you were entitled to (fill in the criminal violation). Everyone will recognize that fact."

The Schizophrenic

Schizophrenics often wander the streets homeless. Schizophrenics make poor witnesses because their thoughts are disorganized and their testimony is easily discredited. If schizophrenics are suspects in criminal investigations, they are more likely than not to talk and will do so by mixing fantasy and realistic thinking.

> *Investigators should not ask schizophrenics leading questions. In time, schizophrenics will provide details that only the criminal would know even though other imagined or invented facts are intertwined. An investigator must exercise patience when interviewing schizophrenics.*

The Antisocial Personality and Psychopaths

People diagnosed with antisocial personality disorder represent about 4 percent of the American population (APA, 1994) and 1 percent of the general population is diagnosed with psychopathy. Psychopaths and make up about 25 percent of maximum prison populations (Hare, 1993). Psychopaths are manipulative and are skilled liars. Psychopaths can also read and assess others with great acumen. Psychopaths are predators and their only concern is about themselves and securing their own agenda. Psychopaths have no morals or ethics and do not tell the truth unless doing so promotes their personal well-being. They admit telling self-serving lies yet manage to endear themselves to the people to whom they lied (Hare, 1993; Meloy, 1988; Kashy & DePaulo, 1996; Gunlicks, 1993).

In the business world, people with antisocial personalities are commonly referred to as Machiavellians. Machiavellians acknowledge that they will do anything, including lie, to attain personal gain (Gunlicks, 1993; Kashy & DePaulo, 1996).

During interviews, psychopaths and people with antisocial personalities appear confident and relaxed and will manipulate and dominate the interviewer if not challenged. Psychopaths dominate the investigator by occupying the interviewer's time and intellect. Psychopaths occupy the interviewer's time by interviewing the interviewer and making self-serving statements. Psychopaths occupy the interviewer's mind with all things except the questions and topics raised by the interviewer.

When interviewing a psychopath, the interviewer should keep the psychopath focused on the question asked. When the psychopath redirects the focus of the question, the interviewer should make a comment to the effect, "That's interesting" and then restate the question. The interviewer should not let the interview continue until the psychopath answers the question posed to the satisfaction of the interviewer.

Psychopaths rarely confess. The most effective way to interview a psychopath is to back him or her into a corner, figuratively speaking, and present several options. When the psychopath realizes that he or she has no way out, the psychopath will pick the option that best serves his or her self-interest.

The Histrionic

The histrionic most often presents in females. Histrionics are impulsive and like to call attention to themselves and are disappointed when they are not the center of attention (APA, 1994). Histrionics typically dress provocatively, flirt with the interviewers, and touch them inappropriately, even suggesting sex (APA, 1994).

Histrionics are more likely than not to talk but have to be constantly focused. Histrionics may feign suicide or self-mutilation and will often cry. Emotional displays should be ignored because histrionics use emotion as a tool to manipulate.

Two individuals should interview histrionics and preferably, one interviewer should be a woman. Histrionics are less successful at manipulating other women as most women see through the histrionic displays and coquettish behavior.

The Paranoid

Paranoids trust no one, and therefore tend to be self-sufficient (APA, 1994). Paranoids continually question the motives of others even though there is no foundation for their suspicions (APA, 1994). Paranoids rarely confide in others (APA, 1994). Paranoids are typically unhappy, argumentative, and hold grudges (APA, 1994). Paranoids perceive threats where none exist (APA, 1994).

Interviewers should always tell the truth when interviewing paranoids. If the paranoid questions the interviewer's motives, the interviewer should ask the paranoid to cite specific examples to support the paranoid's suspicions. Interviewers should avoid getting into arguments with paranoids. Interviewers should focus the interview on the topic of inquiry to avoid hearing a litany of perceived injuries. In most cases, the investigator will have to glean the needed facts from a plethora of information provided by the paranoid.

Establishing

Dominance

Except for special circumstances, the interviewer should establish and maintain dominance throughout the interview even if the interview is conducted in an uncontrolled environment such as the interviewee's home or office. Interviewers should only use dominance techniques when necessary, and symbolic gestures are preferred to violation of personal space; invading personal space elicits negative emotions.

I. The Controlled Interview Environment

Controlling Time

When the suspect arrives at the interviewer's office, make him or her wait at least ten minutes before beginning the interview, especially if an attorney accompanies the suspect (Lewis, 1995). People who are forced to wait on others are placed in submissive roles. Make the suspect and his or her attorney wait 20 minutes if you want to send a strong dominance message.

Controlling Space

The interviewer directs the interviewee to the predetermined chair with an outstretched hand and the verbal directions, "Please, have a seat." If an attorney is present, the interviewer should then direct the attorney to his or her designated chair using the same gesture and verbal command. If the attorney or third party protests, the interviewer has the option of maintaining the status quo or the interviewer could acquiesce and still maintain dominance by saying something to the effect, "On second thought, I've decided to allow you to sit there." This approach forces the attorney or third party to seek permission from the interviewer to sit in a certain chair. The interviewer subtly maintains control of the interview theater without a direct confrontation.

Marking Turf

To ensure that the interviewee and his or her attorney sit in their prearranged seats, place notebooks or other personal items on the chairs designated for the interviewer(s). Interviewees and their attorneys rarely challenge marked turf. If marked turf is challenged, the interviewer simply insists that the person making the challenge take the designated chair because it is more comfortable.

The Last Person Standing

The last person to sit establishes dominance. Let the interviewee and his or her attorney take their seats first. The interviewer should always be the last person standing (Navarro, 2000). The exception to this rule is in military functions where the commander seats first and subordinates follow.

Refreshments

The interviewer should offer those present refreshments. If the offer is accepted, the primary interviewer directs the secondary interviewer to bring the requested refreshments, thus reinforcing the dominance of the primary interviewer.

Cup Position

Providing refreshments to an interviewee serves two purposes. The first purpose is to build rapport. The second purpose is to test for rapport. If the interviewee takes a drink and places the cup, glass, or can in front of the interviewer, rapport has not yet been established because the cup, glass, or can serves as a blocking device. However, if the interviewee takes a drink and places the cup, glass, or can in a position where it does not form a barrier between the interviewer and the interviewee, rapport has been established.

Controlling the Interview Agenda

The interviewer, not the interviewee or his or her attorney, sets the agenda for the interview and introduces the planned topics and themes. If a third-party presents an agenda for the interview, the interviewer should briefly examine the proposed agenda and say, "Thank you. After we discuss the topics I propose, we can address any concerns you may have after our discussion."

Controlling the Interview Pace

The interviewer determines bathroom and smoking breaks as well as breaks for refreshments. Do not allow the interviewee or his or her attorney to dictate these events.

Controlling Breaks

If the interviewee or his or her attorney requests a break, the interviewer could counter by stating, "After I finish the topic we're discussing, we can take a break." The interviewer should talk for at least five minutes before signaling a break.

Controlling Height

The interviewer establishes dominance by sitting in a chair that elevates the interviewer slightly above the interviewee (Pease, 1984). Height advantage should be achieved whenever possible.

Controlling Height

The interviewer who lacks sufficient stature to dominate space can make up for this deficiency by controlling time as illustrated by the twenty-minute waiting rule (Lewis, 1995).

Establish a Parent/Child Relationship

The interviewer should take on the psychological role of the "parent" and relegate the role of the "child" to the interviewee. Conversations take place between equals. The interviewer and the interviewee are not equals. The interviewer takes the parental role at all times, maintaining control, discipline, and authority (Navarro, 2000).

II. Uncontrolled Interview Environments

Controlling space establishes dominance. If the interviewer conducts an interview in the interviewee's office, an environment beyond the interviewer's control, several techniques can establish the interviewer's dominance.

Walk the Walk

Use slow, measured steps when entering an office. Assume the same casual confidence as the rightful owner. Smile and keep an upbeat attitude. Quickly entering an office betrays anxiety and suggests lower status (Lewis, 1995).

Seating Arrangements

An office divides into two sections, private and public. The desk and surrounding area demarcate private space. The placement of chairs, tables, and sofas delineate public space. Higher status visitors sit closer to the desk than lower status visitors (Lewis, 1995; Wainwright, 1993).

Greeting Status

Low-status visitors stay close to the door. High-status visitors approach the desk. A friend is greeted at the door and sits in a chair next to the desk (Wainwright, 1993).

Chair Selection

Avoid chairs and sofas that place the interviewer below the interviewee; height signals dominance. Cushioned furniture often looks sturdy but once sat upon, the investigator sinks, thus trapping him or her in a submissive position. Sit in the sturdiest chair closest to the interviewee's desk, preferably offset to either side of the desk.

Repositioning Furniture

The ideal place to sit in an office places the investigator in a position where no obstacles, including tables and desks, block the interviewer's full view of the interviewee's body. In the uncontrolled interview environment, the interviewee usually sits behind the desk and the interviewer sits in front of the desk. This places the person behind the desk in a position of dominance. The desk also serves as a barrier intended to keep intruders out. The desk also forms a formidable blocking device giving the interviewee a sense of physical and psychological security.

Two techniques can overcome this barrier. The investigator can aggressively assert dominance by moving the chair, if possible, from the front of the desk to either side of the desk. Movement of furniture achieves two purposes: (1) it establishes dominance over private and public office space, and (2) it places the investigator in a position where no barriers block the view of the interviewee. A large portion of non-verbal behaviors emanate from the lower body, not just from the hands and face.

Caveat

Interviewers should reposition furniture with caution because rearranging furniture in another person's office or home sends a powerful message of dominance, often perceived as negative. The interviewer can achieve the same effect by subtly shifting the furniture, thus demonstrating the interviewer's inherent authority.

The Last Person Standing

The interviewer should remain standing until all interview participants seat themselves. In uncontrolled space, this may take some ingenuity. When the interviewee invites the interviewer to sit, the interviewer could comment on a picture or trinket in the office and begin moving in the direction of the object. The interviewer could also feign a sore back and stretch as though loosening the back muscles. The interviewer should execute these maneuvers after the interviewee commits to sitting.

Fully Occupy the Furniture

Occupying space symbolizes dominance (Lewis, 1995). Usurping all available space establishes dominance. Once seated, the interviewer should spread out, lean backwards, and place outstretched arms on the back of the sofa. The interviewer's outstretched elbows dominate space around his or her chair. A strategically placed briefcase can also extend personal space (Lewis, 1995; Pease, 1984).

While seated, high status individuals display dominance by interlacing their fingers behind their heads (Lewis, 1995; Pease, 1984; Nierenberg & Calero, 1971). Interviewers can display a similar gesture to send a strong dominance message.

Invading Private Office Space

Invading private office space establishes or reinforces dominance (Pease, 1984). Personal items displayed in private office space are not readily accessible to visitors. An interviewer invades private office space by walking over to a picture or trinket, picking up the picture or trinket, and complimenting the object. A family photograph presents an optimum target. The interviewer displays dominance and places the interviewee in a socially awkward position. To avoid a confrontation, the investigator should make a comment such as "You sure are lucky to have such a nice looking family" or "I admire a person who takes interest in (describe the trinket being held)." The interviewee can hardly fault the interviewer for making such ingratiating comments (Lewis, 1995). The interviewee cannot challenge the interviewer's comments without disparaging the interviewee's family or favorite interest in the process.

Interviewee: Please, have a seat.

Interviewer: Thank you.

(The interviewer walks toward a free-standing, framed family photograph)

Interviewer: Is this your family?

(Picking up the photograph)

Interviewee: Ye . . . , yes.

Interviewer: (Smiling) You have a very lovely family.

(Replacing the photograph in a slightly different position)

Interviewer: You must be very proud of them.

Usurping Space

An interviewer subtly displays dominance by placing a notebook or briefcase on the desktop at the beginning of the interview. By doing this, the investigator takes control of the other person's personal space. This subtle maneuver signals dominance.

Controlling Time

The Waiting Game

If an interviewee forces an interviewer to wait more than fifteen minutes, the interviewer must reestablish dominance by controlling the interviewee's time. When the interviewee or his or her secretary greets the interviewer, the interviewer politely announces that he or she must return a telephone call. The interviewer then makes a cellular telephone call forcing the interviewee to wait, thus reestablishing dominance (Lewis, 1995).

Busy Work

After fifteen minutes of waiting, the interviewer opens his or her notebook and begins to do some work. When the interviewee or his or her secretary greets the interviewer, the interviewer politely announces that he or she must complete the work at hand. The interviewer then continues to work forcing the interviewee to wait, thus reestablishing dominance (Lewis, 1995).

Departing the Interviewee's Office

When departing the interviewee's office, do not step backwards and then turn to leave. Taking even one step backwards signals submission (Wainwright, 1993). Develop the habit of turning to leave the interviewee's office without taking a step backwards.

Chapter

6

Rapport

I. Building Rapport

Rapport creates trust and builds a psychological bridge between the interviewer and the interviewee (Collins & Miller, 1994; O'Connor & Seymour, 1995; Lieberman, 2000; Rogers, 1961). A person reveals no secrets without rapport.

Rapport building begins with an assessment of the interviewee during the first few minutes of the interview and continues throughout the interview (Zunin & Zunin, 1972). When possible, observe interviewees as they approach the interview location to assess their demeanor and mental state. Social artifacts such as clothing, jewelry, tattoos, and cars are good indications of social status and political ideology (Navarro & Schafer, 2003). The quicker you assess the interviewee, the greater the probability for a successful interview.

Smiling

A smile portrays confidence, happiness, and enthusiasm, but, most important, a smile signals acceptance (Lieberman, 2000; Lowndes, 1999). Smiling also puts the investigator in a better mood, which will enhance his or her interviewing performance (Mueser, Grau, Sussman, & Rosen, 1984; Kleinke, Peterson, & Rutledge, 1998; Wainwright, 1993).

The smile is the most common facial expression and is the easiest expression to recognize (Ekman, 1992; Wainwright, 1993). A sincere smile portrays genuine emotion while a false smile tries to portray a positive feeling when, in reality, this is not the case (Ekman, 1992). A sincere smile differs from a false smile in several ways. With a sincere smile, the cheeks are raised, bagged skin forms under the eyes, crow's feet wrinkles appear around the corners of the eyes, and with some individuals, the nose may dip downward (Ekman, 1992; Saral, 1972).

False smiles are more asymmetrical than sincere smiles and the eyes are not involved. False smiles disappear quickly and may appear noticeably inappropriate (Ekman, 1992). A false smile accompanied by other deceptive nonverbal gestures likely indicate deception (Ekman, 1992; Ekman, Friesen, & O'Sullivan, 1988).

The Art of Smiling

Don't immediately smile when you first meet a person. Pause for a split second, take in the person's face, and then issue full-faced smile. The momentary pause before you issue a smile tells the recipient that your smile was custom made especially for him or her and not just the routine smile issued in public to strangers (Lowndes, 1999).

The Eyebrow Flash

When two people make eye contact, their eyebrows briefly rise and fall (Lewis, 1995; Wainwright, 1993). The eyebrow flash sends the message that people approve of one another and are on good terms (Lewis, 1995). Interviewers should initiate genuine eyebrow flashes whenever possible.

The Head Tilt

A slightly tilted head to either side signals approval. Tilting the head exposes the neck and signals comfort. Head-tilting is often seen during courtship behaviors (Wainwright, 1993).

Names and Formal Titles

Using a person's formal title such as "Doctor," "Professor," "Mister," "Mrs," or "Miss" conveys respect and encourages rapport. In some situations, calling a person by his or her first name can also encourage rapport. Omitting a person's formal title diminishes a person's status and may be useful if the interviewer wants to establish dominance early in the interview. Using names and titles should comport with the interview objectives.

Conversational Encouragers

Head Nodding

Head nodding during conversations signals approval, continued attention, and encourages discourse (Wainwright, 1993). Frequent head nodding during conversations increase the amount of speech by three to four times (Wainwright, 1993; Rogers, 1961).

Verbal Nudges

The interviewer should verbally encourage the interviewee to continue speaking by using simple introjections such as "Uh huh," "yes," "I see," or "go on" (Rogers, 1961).

Mirror Feelings

The empathic statement is the best technique to mirror feelings. The empathic statement is a powerful rapport-building tool. Interviewers should listen to what interviewees say, capture the essence of what they said, and, using parallel language, mirror the same message back to them (Byrne, 1969; Rogers, 1961, Egan, 1975). Empathic statements give the illusion that interviewers understand what the interviewees are thinking and feeling. Empathic statements should focus on the interviewee. The basic formula for constructing empathic statements is "So you (fill in the thought or feeling).

 Interviewee: This is not my day. Things keep going wrong and now this. I can't believe this is happening to me. My life is complicated enough without having to endure this embarrassment. This can't be happening to me.

Interviewer: So you're having a really bad day.

Interviewee: Yeah, I'm having a really bad day. Too much is happening all at one time.

Interviewer: So you're feeling a bit overwhelmed by events.

Interviewee: You got that right.

The Rapport Account

Rapport is similar to a checking account. Before you write a check to purchase something, money has to be in the account. Rapport enables interviewers to ask difficult questions and not alienate interviewees. If an interviewer asks a difficult question and he or she does not have sufficient equity in the rapport account, then rapport diminishes. Prior to asking difficult questions, interviewers should ensure that enough rapport equity has been built to ask the question.

The Handshake

The handshake represents a primary component in impression formation. An inappropriate handshake is unpleasant and can impede your chances for making a good impression (Lewis, 1995). The handshake consists of firmness, duration, style of presentation, eye contact, and body position. Available research suggests that a person's handshake remains consistent over time (Chaplin, Phillips, Brown, Claton, & Stein, 2000). The handshake characteristics described below apply to western cultures. Handshakes vary from culture to culture and interviewers should adjust their handshakes and their assessment of handshake behaviors appropriately.

Firmness

A firm handshake correlates with dominance and aggression (Cecarec & Marke, 1968). Extroverts tend to shake hands with a firmer grip than introverts (Chaplin et al., 2000). Women with firm handshakes demonstrate openness to new experiences; this finding does not apply to men with firm handshakes. A flaccid handshake correlates with shyness and neuroticism (Chaplin et al., 2000). In general, the firmer the handshake, the greater degree of dominance expressed. Friends exert equal pressure when shaking hands (Lewis, 1995; Chaplin et al., 2000). Superiors tend to present firmer handshakes with subordinates.

 To counter an aggressively firm handshake make a habit of placing the web of your thumb squarely into the web of the thumb of the person with whom you are shaking hands. This maneuver prevents the person from applying excessive pressure to your hand. You can master this technique by practicing with a friend.

Duration

The duration of a handshake sends a strong message. The typical handshake lasts from three to five seconds. A quick handshake of (one to two seconds) signals lack of interest and enthusiasm. A long handshake (over five seconds) signals dominance. A handshake lasting slightly longer than normal expresses dominance. An excessively long handshake makes the interviewee feel as though he or she is entrapped (Lewis, 1995).

Style of Presentation

The presentation of the hand reflects a person's orientation. A dominant person typically initiates the handshake by stiffening his arm with the palm facing downward (Pease, 1984; Lewis, 1995). This maneuver forces the other person to turn his or her hand in a palm up position to complete the handshake. The palm up position signals submission (Pease, 1984; Lewis, 1995). If the interviewer wants to display submissiveness, he or she should initiate a palm upward handshake. Vertical hand presentations by both parties represent an equal relationship.

To counter the dominant, palm down handshake, take the person's hand, step forward with your left

*foot and then sideways with your right foot turning
slightly, and enter the person's intimate space (Pease,
1984). Complete the handshake by turning the person's hand to a vertical position and pump the hand
five to seven times (Pease, 1984). Entering the person's intimate space places him or her in a defensive
position, thus countering the person's attempt to
dominate (Pease, 1984).*

Eye Contact

A neutral handshake includes eye contact of normal duration. A
dominant person holds eye contact longer than usual and a submissive
person makes brief eye contact and then glances downward (Wainwright, 1993).

Eye Gaze

Increased eye contact enhances rapport building (Kleinke, 1986;
Kellerman, Lewis, & Laird, 1989; Wainwright, 1993). To increase
rapport, don't break eye contact with the person immediately after
a handshake or greeting, but rather slowly pull your eyes to the
right or to the left (Lowndes, 1999). When one male greets another male, the gaze should be of shorter duration or you might send
the wrong message. With practice, the duration of the eye gaze for
women and for men is easily mastered.

Body Position

A person displaying dominance violates the intimate space of the
person whose hand he or she is shaking (Lewis, 1995; Pease, 1984). For
Americans, intimate space constitutes the area 16 to 18 inches from a
person in all directions (Pease, 1984). Personal space dimensions vary
by geographical regions, ethnic groups, and gender (Navarro, 2000).
Interviewers should learn the personal space dimensions for various
cultures to avoid unintended negative emotions.

The Assertive Handshake

Present a smile and grasp the other person's hand a little longer than
normal and a little firmer than normal (Chaplin et al., 2000; Pease,

1984; Lewis, 1995). Lean slightly forward, maintain eye contact two to three seconds longer than usual, and slowly break eye contact to the left or right but never downward (Lewis, 1995; Pease, 1984).

Third-Party Introductions

Positive or negative words from third parties create the primacy effect, which serves as a filter through which the interviewee views the absent interviewer (Asch, 1946; Edwards & Potter, 1993; Lieberman, 2000; Wainwright, 1993). Early research of first impressions laid the theoretical foundation for the concept of schemas. A schema is defined as "a basic unit of knowledge that develops from past experiences, provides a framework for judging future experiences, and influences how you perceive and react to people and events" (Hock, 1999). When people meet others for the first time, they form first impressions. Thereafter, first impressions serve as filters through which subsequent behaviors are interpreted (Asch, 1946; Lieberman, 2000).

Direct a colleague or the second interviewer to meet with the interviewee alone and introduce into the conversation the desired negative or positive attributes regarding the absent interviewer. The interviewer should also highlight the fact that the absent interviewer is a skilled lie catcher, thus heightening the interviewee's detection apprehension.

 Interviewer: "You're lucky that Detective Peavy is handling your case. He is a fair, open-minded person who takes time to listen to all sides of the story before making any judgments. He is also very good at catching people who don't tell the truth."

Self-introductions

Self-introductions do not produce the primacy effect, but the interviewer can create a positive environment by using positive, uplifting language at the beginning of the interview.

 Interviewer: "I just got back from a fishing trip last weekend. The lake was so calm and the weather was perfect. When the fish weren't biting, I just sat in the boat enjoying the beautiful scenery. The weekend was very peaceful. Well, the reason I want to talk to you is . . ."

Open Posture

Uncrossed legs and arms, palms up displays, and a slight forward lean communicate warmth, trust, and friendliness (Wainwright, 1993). Female interviewers may have an advantage when interviewing men because men are attracted to women who display open postures, lean forward, maintain eye contact, and engage in conversation even if their beliefs and attitudes are dissimilar (Gold, Ryckman, & Mosley, 1984). This is not the case when males interview males. When a male interviewer interviews a male, he should maintain an open posture but be judicious when expressing beliefs and attitudes that are dissimilar to the beliefs and attitudes of the interviewee.

Emotional Flooding

When an investigator confronts a guilty person or a reluctant witness, the person's fight or flight reaction engages (Goleman, 1997). Real or perceived stressors trigger the fight-flight reaction (Rathus, 1994; Golman, 1997; Rudacille, 1994). When the fight-flight reaction initiates, the brain sends signals to prepare the body for survival tactics.

Goleman (1997) describes the body's physiological response to the fight or flight reaction as emotional flooding or the hijacking of the brain. During the fight or flight condition, the brain routes external stimuli directly to the limbic system bypassing the cortex, the part of the brain used for reasoning. Emotional flooding prevents the interviewee from thinking logically; therefore, the investigator should not present any material to the interviewee that requires concentrated thought during emotional flooding. The brain returns to normal functioning after about 20 minutes (Goleman, 1997). Investigators should use this recovery time to build rapport.

Presenting Evidence

When a person is arrested, he or she will likely experience emotional flooding triggered by the fight/flight response. Emotional flooding reduces the ability of the arrestee to think clearly. The interviewer should not expose vital evidence to an interviewee who is emotionally flooded because he or she will not be able to think clearly or process the information. It takes about 20 minutes in a nonthreatening environment for an emotionally flooded interviewee to return to normal. The interviewee should use this 20-minute interval to build rapport. The ride from the place where the interviewee was arrested to the police station can be used to build rapport. Building rapport does not require the arrestee to be Mirandized unless the interviewer directly questions the arrestee about the crime for which he or she was arrested. The interviewer has an assortment of verbal and nonverbal rapport-building tools from which to choose. The combination of nonverbal and verbal techniques helps establish the illusion of a nonthreatening environment.

Seeking Common Ground

Finding common ground quickly establishes rapport (Byrne, 1969; Collins & Miller, 1994; Dalto, Ajzen, & Kaplan, 1979; Lieberman, 2000; Hunt & Price, 2002; O'Connor & Seymour, 1995). Aristotle (350 BC, 1996) wrote, "We like those who resemble us, and are engaged in the same pursuits. . . . We like those who desire the same things as we [do]." Additionally, people beginning conversations with strangers tend to assume that the stranger shares similar beliefs and attitudes, thus making rapport building an easier task (Griffin & Sparks, 1990; Park & Flink, 1989). Commonalities connect the interviewer and the interviewee. Clothing, tattoos, office artifacts, trinkets in the home, or even bumper stickers can reveal common topics of conversation. Identifying a favorite football team, military service affiliations, and other organizational memberships also facilitate finding common ground. Interviewers can seek common ground in three ways:

Contemporaneous Experience
Talking about shared experiences, interests, hobbies, jobs, or any number of other common topics enhances the rapport building process.

Interviewer: "I just started collecting (same objects as the interviewee named). Tell me about your collection."

Temporal Experiences

Experiences shared across time such as attendance at the same school, military experience, or living in the same geographical region enhance the rapport building process.

Interviewer: "I was in the army in the mid-1970s. It sure must have been different from the time when you were in the military."

Interviewer: "Twenty years ago I went to college in the same area where you live. Tell me what it's like now."

Vicarious Experiences

A vicarious experience occurs when you feel the same emotions as a person who engaged in a lifestyle or activity, but you, yourself, have not personally engaged in that lifestyle or activity. Interviewers can use vicarious experiences to establish common ground when they have little in common with the interviewee.

Expressing an interest in a topic in which the interviewee displays a particular interest even though the interviewer has little knowledge or interest can build rapport.

Interviewer: "I've always wanted to have a rose garden in my back yard but I never could get the plants to grow. Tell me how you get your roses to grow so well."

Mirroring Gestures (Isopraxism)

People who share rapport mirror one another's gestures (Rabon, 1994; Lewis, 1995; Lieberman, 2000; O'Connor & Seymour, 1995; Hunt & Price, 2002; Knapp & Hall, 1997; Wainwright, 1993; Pease,

1984). Mirroring the interviewee's gestures is a sign of comfort and helps establish rapport. If the interviewee crosses his or her arms or legs, then the interviewer should cross his or her or arms or legs. If the interviewee leans forward or backward, the interviewer should likewise subtly lean forward or backward.

Creating Suspects

If an interviewer gestures excessively, the interviewee will tend to mirror the interviewer, causing an increase in the interviewee's gestures. The interviewer may judge the interviewee as deceptive because of the increase in the interviewee's gestures (Vrij, Edward, Roberts, & Bull, 2000; Akenjurst & Vrij, 1999; Vrij, 1996). Interviewers must not only catalog the interviewee's behavior but they must monitor their own behavior as well.

Cross Matching

Cross matching simulates the interviewee's behavior without matching gesture for gesture. The interviewer's hand movements can imitate rapid breathing, arm movements, and tapping feet (O'Connor & Seymour, 1995). Head movements can simulate large body movements or shifts in posture (O'Connor & Seymour, 1995).

Mirror Language

The interviewer should use the same words and phrases that the interviewee uses (O'Connor & Seymour, 1995; Wainwright, 1993; Hunt & Price, 2002). People process information by hearing, seeing, touching, smelling, and tasting (Hunt & Price, 2002). Listen to the interviewee's language to determine his or her dominant information-processing medium. Using language that reflects the interviewees' preferred medium builds rapport and encourages them to open up (Hunt & Price, 2002).

Determining Dominant Language Medium

Hearing

The interviewee relies on hearing as a dominant language medium when he or she uses phrases such as: "I *hear* what you are saying"; "It *sounds* like you're trying to tell me this"; "I don't like the *sound* of that"; or "That *sounds* strange."

Sight

The interviewee relies on vision as a dominant language medium when he or she uses phrases such as: "I *see* what's going on here"; "Things aren't *looking* good"; or "I'm beginning to get the *picture*."

Touch

The interviewee relies on touch as a dominant language medium when he or she uses phrases like, "I have a good *feel* for what just happened"; "The story still has a few *rough edges*"; or "I could *feel* the tension in the room."

Smell

The interviewee relies on smell as a dominant language medium when he or she uses phrases such as: "That doesn't pass the stink test"; "I smelled a rat when he told me the story"; "Something just didn't smell right when she told me the story."

Taste

The interviewee relies on taste as a dominant language medium when he or she uses phrases such as: "That story is hard to swallow"; "What happened left a bad taste in my mouth"; or "I nearly choked when I found out."

Mirror Speech Rhythm

Talk slowly if the interviewee talks slowly. Talk fast if the interviewee talks fast.

Mirror Breathing

People tend to mimic one another's breathing patterns. If the interviewer takes slow deep breaths, a nervous interviewee will calm down (O'Connor & Seymour, 1995). The interviewer can calm the interviewee by regulating his or her breathing. If the interviewer slows his or her own breathing, the interviewee will follow suit.

Mirror Dress

People who dress alike usually establish rapport sooner than people whose dress reflects different socioeconomic strata (Wainwright, 1993). The most important aspect of dress is to wear clothes that reflect the image you want to portray during the interview. Wearing a power suit and tie to an interview where the interviewee is wearing a sweatshirt and blue jeans sends a strong dominant message. Matching the dress of the interviewee promotes rapport. Conversely, when an interviewer wears casual dress to interview a CEO, the investigator will put himself or herself at a distinct disadvantage. Decide the image you want to portray and wear clothing that enhances that image.

Touching

Touching indicates a close bond between two people. There is a close correlation between touching and liking (Wainwright, 1993; Dimitrius & Mazzarella, 2000). People typically touch one another when they give advice or information; when they give orders rather than take orders; and when trying to persuade (Wainwright, 1993). Notwithstanding, touching should be used judicially. When strangers meet, the safest place to touch a person is on his or her arms below the shoulders.

Ask a Favor

Ask a small favor of the interviewee. Asking small favors of the interviewee will get him or her to like the interviewer better (Lieberman, 2000; Arnson, 1988; Bigelow, 1916).

Investigator: "Could you do me a favor, look at this organizational chart, and see if it is correct."

Investigator: "Could you do me a favor, lend me your pen for a minute, so I can fill out this form. I only have a pencil."

Flattery

Flattery works; however, people with low self-esteem tend to question the sincerity of the compliment, and therefore, question the sincerity of the person making the comment (Vonk, 2002). To avoid this perception, the interviewer should select a genuinely good quality about the interviewee and make a casual compliment. People like people who flatter them (Clark, Mills, & Corcoran, 1989; Curtis & Miller, 1986; Vonk, 2002; Byrne, 1969). A subtle form of flattery such as addressing the suspect as Mr., Mrs., Miss, or Ms is effective because these titles raise the suspect's self-esteem (Inbau, Reid, & Buckley, 1986).

Allow People to Flatter Themselves

The most effective way to flatter people is to allow them to flatter themselves. This technique avoids the problem of appearing to be insincere when complimenting someone. When people compliment themselves, sincerity is not an issue and people rarely miss an opportunity to flatter themselves.

Investigator: How do you manage to stay in shape with your busy schedule?

Investigator: I'm impressed with the sophisticated planning that went into this crime.

Self-Disclosure

People disclose information to people they like (Collins & Miller, 1994). The tendency to self-disclose can be primed if the interviewer makes personal disclosures at critical junctures during the interview (Collins & Miller, 1994; Wainwright, 1993). If the interviewer discloses information, the interviewee will feel an obligation to reciprocate (Collins & Miller, 1994; Egan, 1975).

Collins and Miller (1994) identified the following levels of self-disclosure: dispositional, situational, and personal. Dispositional self-disclosures occur when someone asks, "How are you?" or "How was your weekend?" Situational self-disclosures derive from physical surroundings or personal circumstances anchored to the environment such as "What do you think of the boss's decision?" Personal disclosures signal a trust relationship with the recipient. Self-disclosure should be at the personal level but the disclosure should not contain intimate details such as personal, financial, or marital troubles. The self-disclosure effect diminishes if the information disclosed is too benign or too intimate. Moderate disclosures garner the best results.

Building Rapport with Victims

Investigators should acknowledge the victim's plight by opening the interview with a statement such as, "I'm sorry for your loss" or "I'm sorry for what happened to you" (Bucqueroux & Carter, 1999). These expressions may seem trite, but at least the victim knows that the investigator is aware of his or her personal suffering.

Although obtaining information is the investigator's chief objective, the victim should be treated with compassion, dignity, and respect (Bucqueroux & Carter, 1999). Investigators should be mindful that victims often suffer from posttraumatic stress syndrome long after the crime occurred.

Secondary Victimization

Secondary victimization occurs when the victim is forced to relive the initial trauma through the interview/investigative process (Bucqueroux & Carter, 1999; Schafer & MacIllwaine, 1992). Investigators should be cognizant that what is routine for them may be horrifying and life changing for a victim. Inquiries should be probative not voyeuristic, especially in rape cases.

II. Testing for Rapport

Good rapport significantly increases the probability of a successful interview outcome. Do not continue the interview without confirming rapport. The following nonverbal gestures test for rapport.

Mirroring Gestures

To test for rapport the interviewer presents a gesture such as crossed legs, a head nod, or a forward lean (Rabon, 1992). If the interviewee mirrors the same gesture, rapport is established and the interview proper can begin. If the interviewee does not respond in like kind, then continue the rapport-building process.

Head Tilting

People tilt their heads to one side or the other when they like someone or hear something favorable. Head tilting is a sign of good rapport (Givens, 2000; Navarro, 2000).

Posture

Forward leaning with arms and legs in an open position signals the establishment of rapport between the interviewer and the interviewee.

Breathing

Normal breathing signals good rapport. Monitor the interviewee's breathing. If the interviewee takes a deep breath periodically, then he or she is not comfortable no matter how calm the interviewee may appear (Lieberman, 2000; Ford, 1996).

Barriers

The placement of soft drink cans, pillows, purses, and other movable objects placed between the interviewee and the interviewer signals discomfort and the lack of rapport. People experiencing good rapport tend to remove extant objects between themselves and the person with whom they are speaking (Navarro, 2000).

Setting Rapport Traps

A combination of the basic rapport-building techniques presented in this chapter can be used to set traps. Interviewees will not be aware of these traps because they mirror the natural behaviors displayed by people who genuinely like each other. The brain only triggers the flight/fight response when it processes behaviors that are outside the human baseline. Since the techniques presented in this chapter are core human behaviors, interviewees will not recognize that they are being manipulated. The advantage of setting rapport traps using core human behaviors is that if they fail, interviewees will be none the wiser because they will not have recognized the traps in the first place. Rapport traps have unlimited upside if they succeed and virtually no downside when they fail. If they do fail, interviewers could simply use a different set of tools. Interviewers who have a wide array of tools in their interviewing tool boxes have an advantage over interviewers who have mastered fewer interviewing tools.

Primacy Effect

Interviewers can predispose interviewees to see the world through the interviewer's perspective by using the Primacy Effect. The Primacy Effect can be established using the Third-Party introduction and to a lesser extent the Self-Introduction. If one interviewer wants the interviewee to see him or her as a human lie detector, the first interviewer describes the absent second interviewer as a human lie detector. When the second interviewer enters the room, the interviewee will view him or her as a human lie detector. The Third-Party Introduction also triggers the Spotlight Effect, which heightens the interviewee's guilt awareness.

The interviewers can use the Primacy Effect to send any number of subtle messages to interviewees. For example, if the interviewer wanted to send the message that the interviewee's codefendant confessed, the interviewer could say, "The train is leaving the station real soon. I don't have any more first class tickets but I can sell you a second class ticket." This Primacy Effect gives the illusion that the interviewer is bargaining from a position of strength, when, in fact, this might not be the case.

The Primacy Effect is a powerful psychological tool. The Primacy Effect does not change reality but, rather, changes the interviewee's perception of reality. The Primacy Effect can be enhanced by the Spotlight Effect. When used properly, the Primacy Effect sets a filter through which the interviewee perceives the interviewer and the interview process.

Make Interviewees Feel Good About Themselves

The quickest way to get someone to like you is to make them feel good about themselves. The focus of the interview should always be on the interviewee. Interviewees who feel good about themselves will attribute that good feeling to the interviewers and consequently build rapport. In long-term relationships, if interviewers make interviewees feel good about themselves, then they will naturally gravitate to the interviewee because they want to replicate the good feeling they feel when they are around the interviewer. Several tools allow interviewees to feel good about themselves. A simple smile says, "I like you." A quick eyebrow flash says, "I like you." A tilted head says, "I like you." Empathic statements say, "I feel the same emotions as you do." Allowing interviewees to flatter themselves makes them feel good about themselves. Asking small favors from interviewees makes them feel good about themselves and consequently builds rapport. Head nodding and verbal nudges say, "I am interested in what the interviewee has to say. These subtle verbal and nonverbal messages predispose interviewees to like their interviewers without the interviewers having to utter a single word.

Get a Commitment to Tell the Truth

People are more likely to adhere to commitments if the commitments are voiced. This technique works in conjunction with Setting High Expectations and Tell a Secret. People tend to live up to expectations of others, especially if they vocalize the commitment. People also feel the need to reciprocate when they receive something of value, no matter how small the value.

> *Investigator: I will make a commitment to you that I will tell you the truth during this interview, no matter what. I need you to make the same commitment to tell me the truth during this interview no matter what. Do I have your commitment?*
> *Interviewee: Yes.*

The interviewee is put in a position where he or she has to make a commitment to tell the truth. If the interviewee refuses, he or she will be placed in a very awkward position. If the interviewee lies at any point during the interview, the interviewer simply reminds the interviewee of the commitment he or she made to tell the truth.

> *Investigator: I thought we had a commitment to tell each other the truth. I haven't lied to you since the interview began. I lived up to my part of the commitment. Why are you having such a hard time living up to your end of the commitment?*

The interviewer could further cement the interviewee's commitment to tell the truth by shaking the interviewee's hand while making the commitment.

> *Investigator: I will make a commit to you that I will tell you the truth during this interview, no matter what. I need you to make the same commitment to tell me the truth during this interview no matter what. Do I have your commitment?*
> *(Interviewer extends his hand to shake the interviewee's hand.)*
> *Interviewee: Yes. (Shaking the interviewer's hand.)*

Arrestee's Psychological Time Line

When a person is arrested, his or her life is in psychological turmoil. The interviewer must help arrestees make sense of their new circumstances. The first thing arrestees want to know is what will happen to them in the present. The interviewer should tell arrestees the specific procedures they will go through, what will happen to their car, who will watch their kids when they are in jail, and any other concerns they might express. After arrestees know what will happen to him in the present, they want to know what will happen to them in the future. The interviewer should tell arrestees what will happen in the future, when they will appear before a judge, will they be able to post bail, and any other concerns they might have. Once arrestees know what will happen to them in the present and in the future, then and only then, can the interviewer go to the past and talk about the actions that brought the arrestees to the present. This technique calms any uncertainties associated with the arrest and gives the illusion that the arrestees are back in control of their lives.

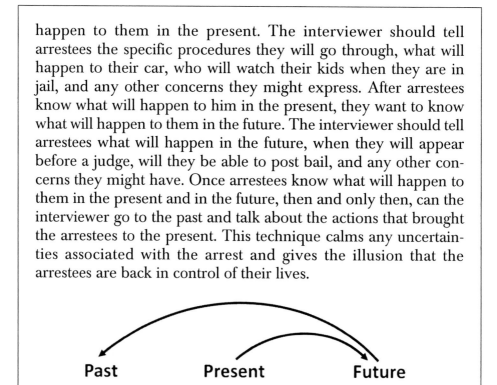

Past   **Present**   **Future**

Anchoring the Message

Associating a message with a gesture or movement serves as a reference to the message without the interviewer having to repeat the message or remind the interviewee what he committed to. Sometimes all it will take is a subtle gesture to remind the interviewee of the interviewer's message or the interviewee' commitment.

Investigator: I will make a commitment to you that I will tell you the truth during this interview, no matter what. (The interviewer begins to deliberately tap a pencil, pen, or other object.) I need you to make the same commitment to tell me the truth during this interview no matter what. Do I have your commitment? (The interviewer stops tapping.)

> *(Interviewer extends his hand to shake the intervie-*
> *wee's hand.)*
> *Interviewee: Yes. (Shaking the interviewer's hand.)*

When the interviewee lies or is suspected of lying to the interviewer, the interviewer repeats the same gesture he or she used when the interviewee made the commitment. Repeating this gesture reminds the interviewee of his or her commitment to tell the truth no matter what. The interviewer does not have to confront the interviewee or call him or her a liar. The gesture will be sufficient admonishment.

Interviewers could also associate a specific gesture with an interview theme or message.

> *Interviewer: As you told me earlier, (The interview-*
> *er begins tapping his or her pen on the table.) this is*
> *all about you being a good father to your kids. (The*
> *interviewer stops tapping the pen.) You have to be*
> *with them to be a good father. When you take respon-*
> *sibility for your actions, you will be with your kids*
> *sooner rather than later.*

The interviewer associated the tapping of the pen with the message ". . . this is all about you being a good father to your kids." If the interviewee needs to be reminded about this message, the interviewer merely taps his pen.

The interviewer included the interview tool Setting High Expectations and the Presumptive to the response. The interviewer stated, "You have to be with them to be a good father." The interviewer set the expectation that a man has to be with his kids in order to be considered a good father. If the interviewee sees himself as a good father, then he will be more motivated to cooperate with the interviewer to be with his kids sooner rather than later. The interviewer provides the interviewee with the method to be with his kids sooner with the presumptive, "When you take responsibility for your actions . . ."

Rapport traps can be set at the same time the interviewer is building rapport with interviewees. The interviewees will not be aware of the traps because the interviewer is operating in the human baseline. A variety of Rapport Traps can be set during the rapport building phase of the interview by combining rapport-building techniques with inter-viewing tools. The only limit to Rapport Traps is the interviewer's imagination.

Miranda Warnings

Investigators often view the reading of Miranda warnings as an unavoidable necessity rather than as a positive interviewing tool. Research demonstrates that four out of five suspects waive their Miranda rights and talk to investigators (Leo, 1996). Miranda warnings, when presented properly, enhance the interview environment and increase the probability of a successful interview outcome. Presenting Miranda warnings after establishing rapport with the interviewee provides the necessary time for the fight or flight reaction to dissipate. Miranda warnings should not interfere with your interview if the interview has been well planned and the suspect is cooperative (willing to talk) even though he or she is guilty and intends to lie about his or her criminal activity.

Caveat

Always check with your organization or legal advisor for your agency's policy on the Miranda warnings.

Miranda Warnings

Remember, the Miranda warnings need not be a "virtual incantation" of the Miranda decision. The only requirement is that the interviewee has a clear understanding of his or her rights (State of California v. Randall James Rysock, 453 U.S. 355, June 29, 1981).

Perception of Control

People who feel in control of their physical and emotional environment tend to communicate more than those people who feel they lack control of their physical and emotional environment (Rhodewalt & Davidson, 1983). The interviewer should use the Miranda warnings as a means to give the interviewee the perception that he or she controls his or her physical and emotional environment.

Investigator: "Before we begin, I'd like to make sure that you understand the guidelines for the interview. First, I'd like to let you know that you are in control of the interview. I can't make you do or say anything you don't want to do or say. You don't have to talk to me unless you want to. You're the boss. You have the power to tell the police to pound sand. That's the kind of power you have right now. If you agree to answer questions, you still have the right to not answer any specific question I ask you. If I ask you a question you don't want to answer, just tell me you don't want to answer the question and we'll move on to the next question. It's very important that you think very carefully about your answers because nothing is off the record and what you say can be used against you in court, so take your time and think about your answers. Remember, just because you agree to talk to me doesn't mean you can't stop the interview at any time and talk to an attorney. If you don't have any money to pay for an attorney, the court will provide an attorney to you at no cost. I want to make sure that you understand what I just told you, so let's go over the guidelines again." (At this juncture, the interviewer presents the interviewee with a written Miranda warnings and waiver of Miranda rights form. The interviewer once again reminds the interviewee that the Miranda guidelines give the interviewee complete control of the interview.)

Do You Think I Need a Lawyer?

If the suspect asks the question, "Do you think I need a lawyer?" the investigator should simply state, "I think you need to tell the truth."

Miranda Waiver

Once the Miranda warnings are given and the suspect signs the waiver, remove the Miranda form from sight and proceed to the next phase of the interview.

The suspect fully understands that he or she can stop the interview at any time. However, establishing good rapport makes that option less probable because the suspect will likely avoid taking any actions that would jeopardize his or her relationship with the interviewer.

Detecting Deception

L ying requires the deceiver to keep facts straight, make the story believable, and withstand scrutiny. When individuals tell the truth, they make every effort to ensure that other people understand. In contrast, liars attempt to manage others' perceptions (Lieberman, 1998; Vrij, 1995; Mitchell, 1996). Consequently, people unwittingly signal deception via nonverbal and verbal cues (Freud, 1905; Ekman, 1992; DePaulo, Stone, & Lassiter, 1985). Unfortunately, no particular nonverbal or verbal cue evinces deception (Ekman, 1992, DePaulo et al., 1985). In fact, multiple studies confirm that lie detection represents a 50/50 proposition, even for experienced investigators (Ekman, 1992; Porter, Campbell, Stapleton, & Brit, 2002; Vrij & Winkel, 1993; Vrij, 1993).

The only certain method of discerning the truth relies on the corroboration of the known facts gleaned independently of the information provided by the person interviewed (Meloy, 1998). Notwithstanding, indirect measures to detect deception such as nonverbal and verbal cues provide investigators with indicators that suggest sensitive topics and the possibility of withheld information (DePaulo, 1994; Vrij, 2001; Vrij, Edward, & Bull, 2001).

Common Mistakes in Detecting Deception

Ekman (1992) identified some common mistakes investigators make when detecting deception:

- Disbelieving the truth and believing a lie.
- Signs of deceit do not always indicate deception.

- The absence of signs of deceit does not always indicate truth.
- A truthful person who feels that he or she is not believed may emit emotions similar to a deceitful person.
- The interviewer believes he or she possesses a special skill to detect deception.

A Two-Stage Process

Detecting deception is a two-stage process. First, the investigator must recognize aberrant verbal and nonverbal behaviors; and second, the investigator must interpret those cues as being indicators of truthfulness or deception (Ekman, Freisen, & O'Sullivan, 1988).

Guilty Knowledge or Guilty Action

Witnesses may display indicators of deception because they fear that interviewers will not believe them (Ekman et al., 1988; Ekman, 1996) or witnesses may withhold embarrassing information not related to the inquiry. Witnesses reluctant to tell the truth display the same, but less intense, verbal and nonverbal cues as liars (Bradley & Rettinger, 1992). With practice, interviewers can discern the differences between reluctant witnesses and suspects withholding information.

A homicide investigator located a witness who adamantly denied any knowledge of a murder. The investigator interviewed the person and detected deceptive behaviors, so the investigator speculated that the person participated in the murder. The homicide investigator later determined that the witness lied not because he took part in the murder but because he was in the company of a prostitute and did not want his wife to find out. The witness feared that if he told the truth about what he saw, his infidelity would be revealed.

Truth Forms a Comprehensive Whole

Truth forms a comprehensive whole. A factual mismatch may give the impression of truth when in actuality it provides a verbal or non-verbal patch to cover a gap in reality. Truth as a comprehensive whole is dynamic in that the truth can become detached from material reality and still give the appearance of truth (Bonhoeffer, 1965).

Liars Described

Liars by definition manipulate others (Ekman, 1992). Introverts lie less frequently than do extroverts (Kashy, & DePaulo, 1996). Liars typically experience less fulfilling same-sex relationships and take responsibilities less seriously than people who lie less frequently (Kashy & DePaulo, 1996). People who prefer socialization as opposed to isolation tend to lie more because social situations often require "little white lies" to maintain social tranquility (Kashy & DePaulo, 1996).

Detection Apprehension

Sane, nonpsychopathic criminals experience deception apprehension (Rudacille, 1994). The criminal not only experiences the guilt associated with committing the criminal act itself but also experiences anxiety when later questioned about the crime (Rudacille, 1994). When an interviewer confronts a guilty person, he or she must evaluate the situation and make a decision to either lie (fight) or be verbally evasive (flight) (Rudacille, 1994). A primary determinant for detection apprehension is the interviewee's perception of the ability of the interviewer to detect lies (Ekman 1992). The greater the perceived ability of the interviewer to catch liars, the greater the detection apprehension manifested (Rudacille, 1994; Ekman, 1992).

Truthful people see the interview as a fact-finding endeavor; liars see the interview as a matter of survival (Rudacille, 1994). The higher the detection apprehension, the more likely it is that the interviewee will leak nonverbal and verbal signs of deception (Ekman, 1992). The interviewer should heighten the interviewee's detection apprehension sufficiently to detect visible signs of deception.

Miller's Law

"In order to understand what a person is telling you, you must first accept that what the person has said is the complete truth, and then ask yourself: What is it true of" (Rudacille, 1994)?

Each person establishes an internal dictionary, which may or may not correspond with material reality (Sapir, 1996). The interviewer must not only obtain facts from the interviewee but must also learn the definitions each interviewee attaches to the words he or she uses (Sapir, 1996). The following exchange between a prosecutor and a forensic pathologist testifying for the defense in a murder trial illustrates the importance of Miller's Law.

Three men beat Milton Walker to death in a vacant lot. A fourth person returned to the scene with one of the three men to determine if Walker died. Finding Walker still breathing, they beat him with a board. The defense attorney for the fourth person postulated that his client was not guilty of murder because Walker was already dead when his client arrived; his client merely hit a corpse. Contradicting extant evidence, the forensic pathologist for the defense testified that Mr. Walker was dead at the time the fourth person struck him. Upon closer examination of the forensic pathologist's testimony, he did, in fact, tell the truth, the truth according to his personal definition of death. After twenty minutes of verbal sparring, the prosecutor discovered the value of Millers' Law when she asked the final series of questions.

Prosecutor: In terms of determining cause of death, you're familiar with the term brain dead?

Expert: Yes, Ma'am.

Prosecutor: Can someone be brain dead but still have heart and lung activity?

Expert: Yes, Ma'am.

Prosecutor: When you say Mr. Walker was dead are you talking about brain dead or are you talking about no heart or lung activity?

Expert: I'm talking about what I consider a clinical brain death.

Prosecutor: So, when you say Mr. Walker was dead for an hour or so, you're talking about brain dead is that correct?

Expert: Yes, Ma'am.

Prosecutor: Mr. Walker still could have had a heartbeat and be dead by your definition?

Expert: Yes.

But I Told You the Truth

When investigators hear the statement, "But I told you the truth," they instinctively reply, "No, you haven't." In the overwhelming majority of the interviews, interviewees do tell the truth. The interviewer must find out the truth about what. The appropriate response to this type of statement is, "Yes, what you told me so far is the truth, I believe you. However, there are many things that you are not telling me. Those things interest me. Tell me some of those things."

The Spotlight Effect

Liars believe others more readily detect their attempts to lie than is the case in reality. Interviewers can take advantage of this "illusion of transparency" by subtly inferring to the interviewee that his or her attempts to lie are readily visible (Gilovich, Savitsky, & Medvec, 1998).

Barriers

Deceivers often use soda cans, computer screens, and other objects, both large and small, to form a barrier between them and the interviewers. Objects used in this manner create distance, separation, and partial concealment–behaviors consistent with dishonesty (Navarro, 2000).

When an interviewee displays a closed posture, he or she is not receptive to input from the interviewer. Before the interview continues, the interviewer must force the interviewee into to a more receptive body posture. An interviewer can either physically remove the blocking device or cause the interviewee to change his or her physical position making the retention of a blocking device such as a purse or pillow uncomfortable. The interviewer can force the interviewee to change positions by asking him or her to look at a document. If the interviewer does not extend the document, the interviewee is forced to move closer to examine the document.

The Four-Domain Model of Detecting Deception[2]

The Four Domain Model simplifies the process of detecting deception by evaluating domains or clusters of behaviors rather than attaching specific meaning to a single nonverbal or verbal display. The Four Domain Model divides communication into four categories: (1) Comfort/Discomfort, (2) Emphasis, (3) Synchrony, and (4) Perception Management. Poor performance in all four domains signals the possibility of deception or, at best, withheld information.

1. Comfort/Discomfort

A person's level of comfort or discomfort is one of the most important clues to establish veracity. People with guilty knowledge show signs of tension and distress because they carry the knowledge of their crimes with them. Attempting to camouflage guilt is stressful because

---

[2] The Four Domain Model of detecting deception was developed by Joe Navarro and presented in a series of lectures at Saint Leo University, Saint Leo, Florida.

liars constantly struggle to fabricate answers to otherwise simple questions and must remember previously fabricated answers (DePaulo, et. al., 1985).

Cues Indicating Comfort

When people are comfortable, they tend to mirror the people with whom they are communicating (Knapp & Hall, 1997). If one person leans forward, the other person leans forward. If one person stands leaning to one side with his or her hands in their pockets and feet crossed, the other person assumes the same position. In this manner, people subconsciously demonstrate their comfort level with others.

Open Posture

Comfortable people display more openly, showing more of their torso and the insides of their arms and legs (Dimitrius & Mazzarella, 2000). Displays of comfort are more common with those who are speaking the truth. Truthful people experience no pressure to hide or conceal information. Guilty knowledge makes most people feel uncomfortable (Ekman & Friesen, 1975).

Removing Obstacles

While seated at a table or desk, people who are comfortable with each other will move objects aside so that nothing blocks their view. Over time, the individuals draw closer so that they do not have to talk as loud. Their breathing rhythm synchronizes as well as their speech intonation, pitch, and general demeanor. These subtleties are important to note in contrast with discomfort.

Cues Indicating Discomfort

People show discomfort when they do not like the environment or the people with whom they are conversing. When people do not like what they are seeing or hearing, or when they are compelled to talk about things they would prefer to keep hidden, they display physiological signs of discomfort such as a quickened heart rate, hairs that stand up, heavier perspiration, and faster breathing.

Fidgeting

Beyond the autonomic physiological responses, people manifest discomfort nonverbally. When people are scared, nervous, or uncomfortable, they tend to move their bodies, rearrange themselves, jiggle their feet, fidget, or drum their fingers (De Becker, 1997; Lowndes, 1999).

Flash Frozen

People who tell the truth may be anxious about the interview but are generally relaxed and display open postures. Guilty people often sit rigidly in a "flash frozen" position indicating discomfort, even though to the untrained eye they may appear comfortable (Knapp & Hall, 1997; Nierenberg & Calero, 1971).

Desire to Leave

When disruptions appeal to the interviewee or the interviewee talks repeatedly about finalizing the interview, discomfort is present. An interviewee who continually looks at his or her watch also signals discomfort.

Distancing Behaviors

When people dislike or are uncomfortable with the people or the things around them, they tend to distance themselves from those people or things. Even while sitting side by side, people will lean away from those with whom they feel uncomfortable. Uncomfortable people will often move their torsos or their feet toward the exit (Knapp & Hall, 1997; Dimitrius & Mazzarella, 2000).

Blocking

People create artificial barriers with their shoulders, arms, or with inanimate objects. In one interview, a very uncomfortable and mendacious interviewee began building a barrier by placing a soda can between himself and the interviewer. Throughout the interview, the interviewee continued to construct his barrier. By the end of the interview, the little barrier grew into a wall of soda cans, a pencil holder, various documents, and a backpack. The interviewee's intent was obvious; yet, the interviewer failed to recognize the symbolism of the objects that lay between him and the interviewee (Navarro, 2000).

Other Gestures Signaling Discomfort

Touching the Head

Rubbing the forehead near the temple region, squeezing the face, neck rubbing, or stroking the back of the head with the hand signals discomfort (Givens, 2000; Pease, 1984).

The Eyes

The eyes serve as a blocking mechanism similar to folded hands across the chest or turning away from disagreeable people or objects. In a similar response, if people hear something disagreeable, they usually close their eyes as if to block out what was just said. The eyes communicate discomfort but these signals often go unnoticed by interviewers.

Interviewers can capitalize on eye blocking behavior by noting when interviewees block with their eyes. Eye blocking is extremely accurate in highlighting problematic areas for the interviewee (Givens, 2000; Navarro, 2000).

Eye Blink Rate

When people are troubled, frustrated, or having silent temper tantrums, their eyelids close or flutter rapidly (Navarro & Schafer, 2001; Knapp & Hall, 1997). In one videotaped interview, close observation determined that the suspect's blink rate increased from 17 times per minute to 84 times a minute during stressful questioning. Conversely, eye blink rates can decrease during intense questioning (Mann, Vrij, & Bull, 2002).

Changes in eye contact and eye blink behaviors are important during interviews. Interviewers should establish the interviewee's normal pattern of eye behavior during benign questioning and then look for changes during critical questions that portend deception.

Misconstruing Eye Movements

The frequency and duration of eye contact and movement varies across cultures (Winkel & Vrij, 1990; Vrij, Dragt, & Koppelaar, 1992). Members of other cultures often avoid eye contact as a sign of respect for authority. Some interviewers erroneously perceive little or no eye contact as a classic sign of deception, especially during intense questioning (Mann, Vrij, & Bull, 2002). Conversely, other people misconstrue direct eye contact during critical questioning as a signal of honesty. However, this is not always the case. Machiavellian people will intentionally increase eye contact to feign honesty (Arthur, 1999).

---

2. Emphasis

When people speak, they naturally incorporate movements of various parts of their body, such as the eyebrows, head, hands, arms, torso, legs, and feet for emphasis. This is important because emphasis is universal when people are genuine. Liars, for the most part, do not emphasize (Lieberman 1998).

Liars think of what to say and how to deceive, but seldom do they think about the presentation of the lie. When people feel compelled to lie, they are not aware of how much emphasis or accentuation enters into everyday conversations.

Emphasis is important for the interviewer because it accurately reflects reality (Ekman & Friesen, 1975). When liars attempt to fabricate an answer, their emphasis looks unnatural or is delayed. Rarely do liars emphasize where appropriate; they typically emphasize unimportant matters.

People accentuate both verbally and nonverbally. Verbally, people emphasize through voice, pitch, tone, or through repetition. People emphasize nonverbally with their arms, legs, head, torso, and hands. In short, the whole body becomes involved in the conversation.

Gesturing for Emphasis

People who use their hands while speaking punctuate their remarks with gestures that emphatically illustrate or exclaim. People accentuate by tapping their fingers, pointing, or pounding their fist on a desk or table. Hand behaviors compliment speech, thoughts, and true sentiments (Knapp & Hall, 1997). The eyebrow flash or widening eyes signal emphasis (Morris, 1985; Knapp & Hall, 1997). People also use their torso to lean forward to show interest or to emphasize.

Gravity Defying Gestures

People employ gravity defying gestures such as rising up on the balls of their feet to make a significant or emotionally charged point. While sitting down, people emphasize by raising and lowering the knees highlighting important points (Navarro, 2000).

Occasionally, people add emphasis by slapping their knee as it rises up, indicative of emotional exuberance. Gravity-defying gestures are emblematic of emphasis and true sentiment, something liars rarely possess.

Lack of Emphasis

In contrast, people de-emphasize or show lack of commitment by covering their mouth with their hand while speaking, or showing limited facial expressions because they are not committed to what they are saying (Knapp & Hall, 1997; Lieberman, 1998; Pease, 1984).

Deceptive people sometimes show pensive displays such as fingers to the chin or stroking their cheeks, as though they are thinking about what to say instead of emphasizing the point they are making (Pease, 1984; Nierenberg & Calero, 1971). Liars evaluate what they say and how they will say it.

3. Synchrony

Ideally, synchrony (i.e., harmony, congruence) exists between the interviewer and the interviewee, between what is being said verbally and nonverbally, between the circumstances of the moment and what the subject is saying, and between events and emotions, including synchrony of time and space (Wainwright, 1993).

In an interview setting, the tone voice of the interviewer and the tone of voice of the interviewee should mirror each other over time if there is synchrony (Cialdini, 1993). Synchrony in speech patterns, sitting styles, touching frequency, and general expressions should also manifest.

When the interviewer and the interviewee are out of "synch," they sit apart, talk in a manner or tone different from one other, and their expressions will be at odds if not totally disparate. Lack of synchrony is a barrier to effective communication, an essential component of honesty.

Head Movements

When being interviewed, a person answering in the affirmative should display a congruent, nondelayed, head movement corresponding to what he or she just said. Lack of synchrony is often found when people say, "I did not do it," while their heads nod up and down as if saying, "Yes, I did." When asked, "Would you lie about this?" their heads bob up and down while they say, "No." Upon catching themselves in this *faux pas*, they will attempt to reverse their head movements making the lack of synchrony more obvious.

Liars delay their answer and use less emphatic negative head movement following a mendacious statement such as, "I did not do it." These behaviors are asynchronous and therefore more likely indicate lying.

Synchrony between what people say and the events of the moment should be obvious. During an interview, the interjection of extraneous information or irrelevant facts by the interviewee should alert the investigator to disharmony. The information and facts should be relevant to the circumstances, and the questions asked. When the answers are asynchronous with the event and questions, something is likely wrong or the person is stalling to fabricate a story.

 When a person reports the alleged kidnapping of their infant, synchrony should exist between the event (kidnapping) and the emotions of the person reporting the crime. The complainant should be clamoring for law enforcement assistance, emphasizing every detail, feeling the depth of despair, eager to help, and willing to tell and retell the story, even at personal risk. When such reports are made by placid individuals who are more concerned with getting one particular version of the story out, lacking consistent emotional displays, or more concerned about their own well-being and how they are perceived vis-à-vis the egregious event (alleged kidnapping of a loved one), this is totally out of synchrony with circumstances and inconsistent with honesty.

Spatial-Temporal Synchrony

Synchrony (congruence) should exist among events, time, and space. A person who delays reporting a significant event, such as the drowning of a fellow passenger, or a person who travels to another jurisdiction to report an event, should rightfully come under suspicion, as should the reporting of events that would have been impossible to observe from the vantage point from which the story is being told. People who lie do not think about how synchrony fits into the presentation of facts and events.

4. Perception Management

Liars must plan how to tell lies and manage their behavior to avoid detection (Vrij, 1995; Mitchell, 1996). Perception management becomes significant during interviews because liars attempt to mislead interviewers. Nonverbally, subjects will yawn excessively as if to show that they are bored and unperturbed by the inquiry. Liars will often slouch or splay out on a couch, extending their arms to cover more territory, giving the perception of comfort.

Verbally, liars will try to vocalize their honesty, integrity, and the implausibility of their involvement in the commission of a crime. Liars try to "look good" to the interviewer. Prevaricators may use perception management statements such as, "I could never hurt someone," "Lying is below me," "I have never lied," "I would never lie," or "I would never do such a thing," which should alert investigators to the possibility of deception. Other statements such as "to be perfectly frank . . . ," "to be honest . . . ," "to be perfectly truthful . . . ," or "I was always taught to tell the truth," are solely intended to influence the perception of the interviewer (Lieberman 1998).

Other forms of perception management include the interviewee bringing someone of prominence in the community to the interview or dropping the names of so-called "high officials" at strategic intervals throughout the interview. Also, the liar may self-medicate with alcohol or prescription drugs in order to appear relaxed. Liars may change their clothing or hairstyles in order to look more genuine or in an attempt to appear more socially conventional.

Summary of the Four Domain Model of Deception

Detecting deception is a difficult task. Interviewers can enhance their ability to detect deception by focusing on the four domains, (1) Comfort/Discomfort, (2) Emphasis, (3) Synchrony, and (4) Perception Management, rather than merely trying to detect traditional signs of deception that, in some cases, may be misleading (Ekman, 1992).

Research over the past 20 years is unequivocal. There are no verbal or nonverbal behaviors that, in and of themselves, clearly indicate deception (Ekman, 1992; Ford, 1996). However, if an investigator uses the Four Domain Model, a general baseline for veracity can be established by evaluating the four critical areas: comfort/discomfort, emphasis, synchrony, and perception management (Navarro, 2002). Poor performance in one or two domains is not unusual, but poor performance in all four domains is indicative of communication problems at best. These problems may originate from the interviewee's antipathy toward the interviewer, from disdain for law enforcement, from culpability, or it may simply be the unwanted and inconvenient residue of lying.

Nonverbal

Behavior

Approximately 60 to 80 percent of communication is nonverbal; therefore, being able to read people is crucial to interviewing (Lowndes, 1999; Berry & Landry, 1997). Investigators often overlook behavior *leakage* when evaluating interviewees (Burgoon et al., 1999) or try to interpret a single behavior instead of viewing clusters of nonverbal behaviors. Nonverbal communication errors also occur when an interviewer is from one culture and the witness or suspect is from another culture (Vrij, Dragt, & Koppelaar, 1992; Vrij, 1997a). Establishing baseline behaviors is critical when conducting cross-cultural interviews.

Proxemics

Proxemics is a term coined by Hall (1966) to differentiate intimate, personal, social, and public distances. Personal space varies by culture and gender but typically extends from 18 inches to three feet around an individual (Hall, 1966). The interviewer should norm the interviewee for spatial preferences during the interview. Violating the interviewee's personal space is stressful and works against the interviewer if the intrusion is unintentional. Violating personal space increases tension and should only be used in conjunction with a global interview strategy.

Territorial Displays

Claiming territory by spreading one's arms over a chair or placing property around oneself is a display of comfort and superiority (Nierenberg & Calero, 1971; Pease, 1984). Even putting hands on the hips with elbows sticking out (arms akimbo), is territorial, as is standing with legs spread apart (Givens, 2000).

Sitting Displays

Withdrawing into the comfort of a chair or assuming the fetal position is a sign of weakening resolve and withdrawal. A partial fetal position, pulling the knee up with wrapped arms around one or both shins, also indicates discomfort and withdrawal.

Stance

Stance displays demonstrate authority or subordination, confrontation or cooperation, indifference or concern, restlessness or contentment; be careful what message you send (Lewis, 1995; Nierenberg & Calero, 1971). An open stance, legs spread apart, signals dominance. A closed stance, heels touching, signals submission. The wider the stance, the more confrontational the interviewee is likely to be.

Staring

How people stare at others and the length of time that they stare can demonstrate subordination, superiority, or even intimidation. The longer the stare, the more dominance is displayed (Strom & Buck, 1979; Lewis, 1995; Givens, 2000). Looking down is a sign of subordination and submission.

The Power Stare

To send a dominance message, the interviewer should continue to look at the interviewee even when a second interviewer is talking. This gesture sends a powerful message. To send a less powerful but still effective message, look at the other investigator while he or she is speaking and then, when the investigator stops talking, look immediately at the interviewee (Lowndes, 1999).

Posture

Posture demonstrates vitality, eagerness, and capability, or it can show lack of enthusiasm, illness, incompetence, or worse, serve as a detractor (Lewis, 1995). Liars show an overall decrease in hand, finger, feet, and leg movements (DePaulo, Charlton, Cooper, Lindsay, & Muhlenbruck, 1997; DePaulo et al., 1985; Vrij et al., 2000).

Attire

The careful choice of clothing allows the interviewer to formalize or relax an interview (Dimitrius & Mazzarella, 2000). Clothing also creates a superior versus inferior relationship with someone depending on the interview objectives. A dark blue suit, white shirt, and a conservative tie can project success, competency, and even veracity (Molloy, 1975). Conversely, a suspect who wears dark clothing, especially black clothing, evokes a more aggressive impression and is seen as more likely to be guilty (Vrij, 1997b).

Symbols and Emblems

Clothing, ornaments, jewelry, tattoos, and other emblems reveal a how a person sees the world and how people want the world to see them (Navarro & Schafer, 2003; Pease, 1984). Symbols and emblems also indicate a person's affiliations and beliefs, as well as the extent to which the person adheres to social conventions (Morris, 1980).

Eyes

The eyes often communicate when the brain is processing information, conducting internal dialogs, recalling past events, crafting answers, or conducting concentrated thinking. Eye movement should be "normed" when the interviewee answers benign questions and the normed responses should then be compared to eye movements when critical questions are asked (Navarro, 2000).

Eye Blocking

Eye blocking is similar to people positioning their arms across their chest or turning away from disagreeable people (Pease, 1984; Nierenberg & Calero, 1971). People who do not like what they hear tend to close their eyes as if to block out what they just heard. Eye closure may be followed by finger stroking of the eye as if to further block what was heard (Nierenberg & Calero, 1971). Investigators can capitalize on these subconscious gestures by noting when interviewees block with their eyes, an indication that the question or topic is troublesome.

Eyelid Flutter

When some individuals become frustrated or dislike something they just heard, their eyelids often flutter rapidly reflecting consternation or frustration. Eyelid flutter is a very accurate and immediate indicator of stress (Givens, 2000).

Eye Rolling

Some people will roll their eyes as an expression of their incredulity or disrespect.

Eye Blink

People under stress blink their eyes more often (Knapp & Hall, 1997). However, stress should not automatically be equated with lying.

Lip Biting

Biting down hard on the lip is indicative of stress or, if done softly, it can indicate someone is ready to speak. If it is the latter, stop and ask the interviewee if he or she has something to say; he or she usually does.

Mouth Quiver

Mouth quivering is a sign of nervousness or stress.

Throat Clearing

Liars sometimes clear their throats. The fight/flight response causes the need for throat clearing because the moisture usually present in the throat has be rerouted to the skin to enhance survivability.

Facial Touching

For years, facial touching was associated with deception (Ekman & O'Sullivan, 1991; Kraut, 1978; Fiedler & Walka, 1993). However, anecdotal evidence suggests that both honest people and dishonest people touch their faces during interviews. Facial touching must be evaluated in conjunction with other nonverbal behaviors.

Hand to Neck

Touching any part of the neck is usually an indicator of something troubling, bothersome, or of concern (Pease, 1984; Nierenberg & Calero, 1971). Deceptive interviewees often touch their necks following difficult questions.

Hand to Cheek

Hands to cheek gestures or hand to chin gestures are indicators suggesting evaluation. However, the chin resting flat on palm of hand more likely indicates boredom (Nierenberg & Calero, 1971).

Hands to Chest

A hand to the chest gesture when speaking suggests the speaker is committed to the statements that he or she is voicing (Nierenberg & Calero, 1971). This gesture is a general indication that a person is truthful.

Suparsternal Notch

The suprasternal notch is the indentation at the base of the throat. The suprasternal notch represents one of the most vulnerable parts of the body. When liars feel threatened they sometimes cover their suprasternal notch to protect themselves against a real or perceived threat.

Palms Up

Gesturing with palms up generally indicates openness; the interviewee has nothing to hide (Pease, 1984). A palms up gesture is a more likely indication of truthfulness.

Interlaced Fingers

Hands clenched together with fingers interlaced is a gesture of frustration (Nierenbrg & Calero, 1971; Pease, 1984; Ekman & Sullivan, 1991; Dimitrius & Mazzarella, 1999). When seated, the fingers interlaced gesture takes two forms, hands elevated in front of the face with elbows resting on the table, or hands resting on the table. When standing the crossed fingers typically hang in front of the person's body (Pease, 1984). The higher the elevation of the crossed fingers, the more negative the person's mood (Pease, 1984).

Partial Smiles

Partial smiles, indicative of stress, are often seen during deception (Ekman, 1992; Saral, 1972).

Arm Block

Bringing one or both arms across the chest is a sign of discomfort and withdrawal. Turning away or pointing the feet towards an exit often follow the arm block gesture (Lewis, 1995; Nierenberg & Calero, 1971; Dimitrius & Mazzarella, 1999).

Hands on Armrests

A person who holds a chair's armrest while leaning forward signals a desire to leave or is feeling discomfort (Navarro, 2000).

Illustrators

When describing actions, truthful people tend to use their hands to illustrate or act out the words they speak. Liars cannot act out the words they speak because they did not do the things they are describing. Liars often mix the truth with deception, so the presence of illustrators does not always signal truthfulness.

Pacifying Gestures

Pacifying gestures include stroking the hair, face, lips, neck, thighs, or other parts of the body. Liars use pacifying gestures to calm themselves.

Grooming and Preening

Grooming and preening gestures such as picking lint off one's clothing during an interview is a display of indifference, boredom, or disrespect (Pease, 1984).

Crossed Legs

Crossed legs is a blocking gesture indicating discomfort. When a crossed leg begins to kick, it means the interviewee does not like the question or topic (Pease, 1984).

Feet Pointing

A comfortable interviewee should point their feet toward the interviewer. Feet pointed towards the exit likely indicate discomfort (Navarro, 2000; Dimitrius & Mazzarella, 1999).

Jittery Feet

Jiggling one's legs may be a sign of stress or nervousness, discomfort, anxiousness, or a desire to leave.

Assurance and Confidence

A steepling gesture (fingers of the hands pressed together like a church steeple) is a sign of confidence, assurance, and sometimes arrogance (Lewis, 1995). Steepling can also be used as a blocking gesture when the interviewee's clasped hands are positioned directly between the interviewee and the interviewer. The steepling gesture used as a blocking mechanism presents a formidable obstacle for the interviewer to overcome.

Emphasis

Gravity defying gestures such as rising up on toes and raising an eyebrow are used as emphatic gestures. Rarely do liars use emphatic gestures because they are not committed to their statements. People who tell the truth typically use emphatic gestures such as touching and pointing.

Body Inclination

People tend to lean towards those with whom they are comfortable. When uncomfortable, people lean away from those they dislike or toward the exit (Nierenberg & Calero, 1971).

Posture

People who tell the truth reflect openness in their posture. The more ventral (frontal) posture the person displays, the more comfortable the person feels. Arms out in front, palms up, is an often-used display of openness. When people begin to block their ventral aspect with crossed arms, by turning, or by placing objects in front (purse, pitcher of water, table objects, even additional clothing), it is reasonable to conclude that the person is putting up barriers due to discomfort with the situation or with what is being uttered. Barriers often serve as security for people who are afraid, insecure, threatened, or are in the process of lying (Navarro, 2000).

First Look

Liars typically reveal their real reactions to anxiety-provoking questions of statements within the first second of hearing the question. The First Look is critical because this may be the only time officers see an interviewee's real feelings and reactions. The First Look is effective, especially during traffic stops. Upon seeing the driver, the officer should inwardly ask, "Is this a person I don't have to worry about or is this person someone I should take a closer look at?" Interviewers' initial impressions are usually correct.

Cognitive Load

Cognitive loading causes the brain to concentrate on a problem, issue, or memory to the exclusion of other thoughts. A sudden or unexpected change in countenance after a critical question is asked reveals that the question placed a cognitive load on the person, causing him or her to think deeply about the answer (Depaulo, 1992; Ford, 1996; Elliot, 1979). Interviewees usually deflect such questions by saying, "Please repeat the question" to give them additional time to formulate their answer.

Verbal Clues to

Deception

I. Clues to Detect Deception

Liars know the truth but must alter the facts in a manner that will make their version of events believable. Liars make more speech hesitations and speech errors, have higher pitched voices, wait longer before giving an answer, and pause more often when they speak (Ekman, Freisen, & Scherer, 1979; Knapp & Comadena, 1977; Vrij et al., 2001). Truthful people do not require extra time to alter the facts; therefore, they answer the question in less time than a liar would need to answer the same question. A liar hesitates before answering a question in order to reconstruct sentences to convey the opposite meaning and to decide how to present the altered statements as well as evaluate how others will perceive the altered statements (Vrij, 1995). Additionally, the liar must attach the appropriate emotional tag, a step often overlooked (Ekman, 1992).

Convince or Convey

Liars try to convince others that they are telling the truth; truthful people merely convey facts. Truthful people tend to go on the offensive when they are falsely accused and liars tend to become defensive when they are confronted. Caution should be used when applying this general rule of thumb. Liars tend to "Shout their message" to make sure the interviewer gets the intended communication.

Be a Skeptic

When liars are exposed to skepticism, they believe that their statements lack credibility. Consequently, liars try even harder to convince the interviewer that the statements are truthful (Burgoon, Buller, White, Afifi, & Buslig, 1999). The harder liars try to manage the perception of the interviewer, the more mistakes liars are apt to make. However, with sufficient practice, liars can assimilate verbal and nonverbal behaviors similar to a person who is telling the truth (Burgoon & Floyd, 2000; Granhag & Stromwall, 2001).

Positive Verbal and Nonverbal Signals

Reward wanted behavior with positive verbal and nonverbal signals. When the interviewee cooperates, accelerate the rate of conversational encouragers such as head nodding and smiling, and at the same time lean toward the interviewee.

Negative Verbal and Nonverbal Signals

Discourage unwanted behavior with negative verbal and nonverbal signals. When the interviewee does not cooperate, cease or significantly reduce conversational encouragers, stiffen your countenance, and lean backwards away from the interviewee. To send an even stronger message the interviewer should cross his or her arms and legs.

Converting a Positive Statement

The quickest and easiest way to construct a lie is to make a positive statement negative. Question: "Did you steal the money?" Conversion: "No, I did not steal the money." The guilty person responds quickly to avoid giving the impression of a delayed answer, which signals deception (Dulaney, 1982). A variation of this ploy occurs when a person answers "yes" or "no" immediately, but the explanation comes more slowly because the liar needs time to construct a plausible answer (Lieberman, 1998).

Verb Tense

Verb tense changes suggest deception (Dulaney, 1982; Rudacille, 1994; Sapir, 1996). When a person tells the truth, he or she recalls events from the past and appropriately relates those events in the past tense. A liar must alter the truth, which occurred in the past, and construct a lie. To accomplish this task, the liar reconstructs the events in his or her mind in the present tense omitting incriminating information. Next, the liar must convert the fabricated events, which are thoughts in the present tense to the past tense, thus giving the impression that the events occurred prior to the interview. Liars successfully accomplish this task most of the time but not all the time. The interviewers should listen carefully to verb tense changes because they indicate that the person is describing fictional events imagined in the present, instead of relating actual events that occurred in the past.

Another theory posits that deceivers use the present tense to keep the focus of the interview in the present rather than on past events, which the deceiver wants to avoid. By focusing on the present, the interviewee naturally uses fewer past tense verbs (Dulaney, 1982).

*A store clerk suspected of theft stated: "I <u>closed</u> the cash register at about 10 o'clock. I <u>took</u> my drawer to the back room and **count** the receipts. I **see** there are six $100 dollar bills. I **place** the bills in the moneybag. I <u>sealed</u> the bag, <u>dropped</u> it in the drop box, and went home." The point in the narrative when the clerk started using the present tense is probably the point where the theft occurred. In this example, the investigator should focus on the time the clerk spent in the backroom.*

Passive Voice

Deceptive people use the passive voice more frequently than people who tell the truth (Dulaney, 1982; Rudacille, 1994; Sapir, 1996). The active voice emphasizes the subject. For example, John killed the bank teller during the robbery. John took an active role in killing the bank teller. The passive voice gives the impression that the subject received the action. For example, the bank teller was killed by John. The bank teller is the recipient of the action performed by John. The emphasis is on the bank teller, not John. The passive voice psychologically distances the suspect from the activity in question. The use of a passive voice does not, in and of itself, indicate deception. For example, John was found murdered in his home. During the police interview of his wife she said, "John was shot by someone." The use of the passive voice could indicate that John's wife distanced herself from his death because she was somehow responsible for his death. The use of the passive voice could also mean that she distanced herself from John's death because she loved him and wanted to distance herself from the emotional pain or reality of the death of a loved one.

Prepositions

Deceptive people seldom use prepositions or prepositional phrases (Lieberman, 1998). Pennebaker, Matthias, & Niederhoffer, 2003). The use of prepositions requires more cognitive processing. Since liars use most of their cognitive processing trying to keep track of their lies, they tend to use less complicated grammar structures.

Articles

The articles "a" or "an" identify a nonspecific person, place, or thing (e.g., a car, a gun, a man) (Flemons, 1998). When "a woman" is used, the speaker has not yet been introduced to the woman. The article "the" identifies a specific person, place, or thing known to the speaker. When "the woman" is used, the speaker has already been introduced to the woman. The use of articles can be important in rape cases. The statement "A man raped me" is very different from the statement "The man raped me." In the first case, the woman does not know the man. In the second case, the woman has had some prior acquaintance with the man, however distant, on a previous occasion or there was a time lapse between the first contact with the rapist and the rape.

Articles can also signify plurality. The statement, "I grabbed a gun from my car" suggests that more than one gun was in the car. Conversely, the statement "I grabbed the gun from my car" suggests that only one gun was in the car.

Pronouns

Pronouns provide a powerful tool to confirm the truth or uncover deceit.

We

The pronoun "we" signals mutual association (Sapir, 1996). In a rape case, the supposed victim wrote, "We went into the alley where he raped me." The pronoun "we" suggests that the victim willingly went into the alley with the accused rapist, a person the victim probably knows.

The pronoun "we" can also determine the intensity of a relationship. An interviewee wrote "Mary and I entered the restaurant for lunch and after lunch, we went back to work." The two people entered the restaurant as individuals (Mary and I) and they exited the restaurant together (we went back to work). This statement suggests that something happened in the restaurant to make the interviewee feel he had a closer relationship with Mary.

My

The pronoun "my" indicates possession. Deceitful people rarely use the pronoun "my" in association with instruments of a crime or things associated with the crime (Rudacille, 1994; Sapir, 1996). For example, in an espionage investigation the interviewee stated, "I took my radio, my tape player, my tapes, and the palm pilot out of my trunk." The interviewee dissociated himself from the palm pilot. Based on this observation, the interviewer used the presumptive technique and told the interviewee that he knew that the interviewee had illegally downloaded classified information onto his palm pilot. The interviewee, thinking the interviewer knew all the facts, provided a full confession.

Introjections

Truthful people use introjections such as "Oh," "Yeah," or "Well" to signal a sudden thought or a fact retrieved from long-term memory. Deceitful people use introjections to give themselves time to evaluate how to answer the question or time to concoct an acceptable answer (Rudacille, 1994).

Indirect Answers

A liar typically provides an indirect answer to a direct question. The indirect answer often incorporates responses such as, "My mother taught me to always tell the truth," "I'm not the kind of person who lies," "That's an excellent question," "I would never do such a thing," or "I'm a religious person." Other statements such as "to be perfectly frank . . . , "to be honest . . . ," "to be perfectly truthful . . . ," or "I always tell the truth" often intend to deceive.

Speech Interrupters

When the interviewee uses speech interrupters such as "Uh," "Ah," "Err," "Um," with no reasonable explanation, the likelihood the interviewee is lying increases if the speech pattern is different from baseline behavior (Eckman, 1992; Hirsch & Wolf, 2001; Depaulo, 1992).

Contractions

Liars often avoid using contractions. For example, a truthful person tends to use the contracted form "I wasn't there," while a liar tends to expand the contraction, "I was not there," emphasizing the word "not" (Lieberman, 1998; Hirsch & Wolf, 2001). However, anecdotal evidence suggests that honest people will also use expanded contractions in an effort to convince a disbelieving interviewer. In either case, the expanded contraction should be explored in more detail by the interviewer.

Voice Pitch

Liars, in general, raise the pitch of their voice when engaged in deception (Ekman et al., 1979; Ekman, 1992; Knapp & Comadena, 1977). However, some liars decrease the pitch of their voice when lying (Canter & Alison, 1999). The best way to gauge changes in the interviewee's voice is to establish a baseline during the rapport-building portion of the interview.

Details

Truthful people sometimes offer more details than liars when relating events. Details should not be confused with extraneous information that has nothing to do with the event being described. Extraneous information can signal deception.

Negative Events

Truthful people relate the negative as well as the positive events in their stories. Liars rarely include negative details (Lieberman, 1998).

Text Bridges

Most liars tell the truth up to the point where they want to conceal information, skip over the withheld information, and tell the truth again. Successful liars construct sentences that allow them to skip over withheld information to make the story appear truthful. Constructing a sentence to span the information gap replicates building a bridge across a river. A road stops at the river's edge, a bridge spans the river, and the road continues on the opposite bank. Bridges come in a variety of designs, but each design must adhere to specific construction standards or structural failure occurs. Likewise, sentence construction must follow certain grammar rules. Isolating the words or grammatical devices used to bridge information gaps identify intentionally or unintentionally withheld information. The grammatical devices used to bridge information gaps, also referred to as Text Bridges, serve as markers to locate withheld information; however, withheld information does not always indicate deception.

Text Bridges allow people to transition from one topic to another without detailing tedious, lesser-included activities. For example, in the sentence "I got up, and then I took a shower, and then I ate breakfast," the Text Bridge *then* signals withheld information. The withheld information does not constitute deception. The communicator did not want to bore the listener or reader with the lesser-included activities of taking a shower and eating breakfast. The omitted activities encompass turning on the water, soaping, rinsing, drying off, donning clothes, walking to the kitchen, taking a bowl from the cupboard, filling the bowl with cereal, going to the refrigerator to get milk, etc. However,

Text Bridges used at critical times during interviews or interrogations may signal deception. Investigators must assess the potential value of the missing information. If investigators deem the missing information to have no value, then they can ignore the Text Bridge.

The most commonly used Text Bridges include *then, so, after, when, as, while,* and *next.* This easily memorized list of Text Bridges provides a powerful tool to identify where people withhold information during interviews. The following illustration demonstrates how Text Bridges can be exploited. A student wrote a statement in response to an allegation that she took $20 from her professor's office during the first class break. Pursuant to an informal investigation, the student wrote a narrative account of her activities from the time she entered the building until the end of the first break. The following is a copy of her statement:

> I arrived at 7:45 a.m. with Jenna. I came into the room, put my bag at my desk and Jenna and I went to the little snack area to get some coffee. I returned to the classroom and sat at my desk. At 8:50 we went on a break. Jenna and I went to the bathroom. After that I came back to the classroom and Jenna stayed in the bathroom. She came back to the classroom soon after. We sat at our desk and waited for our class to continue.

The critical time in the narrative is at the first class break when the $20 was taken. The section of the narrative that addressed the break is, "At 8:50 we went on a break. Jenna and I went to the bathroom. After that I came back to the classroom and Jenna stayed in the bathroom. She came back to the classroom soon after." The student used the Text Bridge *after* which created an information gap from the time she went to the bathroom and to the time she came back to the classroom. This information gap in the student's narrative covered the time she walked to the instructor's office and stole the $20. After conducting a Micro-action Interview, the student admitted taking the $20. Micro-action Interviews will be discussed later in this book. The student used the Text Bridge *after* to conceal the fact that after she went to the bathroom and before she returned to the classroom she walked down the hall to the instructor's office and stole $20. In addition to the use of a Text Bridge, the student misdirected the reader. The student was asked to provide an account of *her* activities not Jenna's activities. The student focused on Jenna's activities to substitute for the missing time when the money was stolen.

Text Bridges do not necessarily indicate deception. Both liars and truthful people use Text Bridges. Text Bridges signal missing information. Investigators must decide if the missing information has value. Missing information during critical times should always be pursued. Obtaining missing information before or after the offense is at the investigator's discretion

Spontaneous Negations

When people respond to open-ended questions, they should describe the actions they took rather than the actions they did not take. The use of Spontaneous Negations indicates a high probability of deception. Spontaneous Negations differ from negations in that negations are used in response to direct questions. For example, "Did you rob the bank?" a deceptive person as well as a truthful person would answer, "No, I did not rob the bank." Spontaneous Negations occur during narrative answers or in response to open-ended questions. Spontaneous negations used during open-ended questions may provide additional cues to differentiate truthful narratives from deceptive narratives, especially when they are used in conjunction with Text Bridges.

Interviewer: I see that you've been in the United States for eight months. I hope you had time to do some sightseeing.

Interviewee: Yes, I visited California, Utah, and Texas, but I never visited New York.

The use of the Spontaneous Negation *I never visited New York* indicates a high probability that the interviewee, in fact, visited New York. Of the 47 states the interviewee did not visit, he singled out New York as a state he did not visit for a reason. The use of Spontaneous Negations signal a high probability of deception.

Stalling Ploys

Repeating the Question

Liars typically ask investigators to repeat questions without realizing that honest conversations do not require the restatement of questions. Restating questions gives the witness/suspect additional time to formulate a plausible answer (Walters, 2000).

Delaying Phrases

The following responses provide liars with additional time to formulate his or her answer: "It depends on what you mean," "Where did you hear that?" "That's a good question," "Where are you getting your information?" "Could you be more specific?" and "Well, it's not so simple as "yes" or "no."

A Doggie Biscuit Instead of a Bone

A suspect often provide investigators with small admissions, usually lesser-included offenses or alternate explanation, to give the investigator the impression that the suspect if making a full confession. Interviewers should always make further inquiry to determine if the minor admissions are masking greater involvement by the suspect.

Loss of Memory

People forget trivial matters in their lives. People do not forget significant events. Responses such as "I don't remember"; "I can't recall"; or "Not to the best of my recollection" may suggest deception. In order for a person not to remember, not to recall, or not to recollect, the person would first have to remember, recall and to recollect what has been ostensibly forgotten (Sapir, 1996; Walters, 2000). Truthful people typically answer, "I don't know."

II. Testing the Truth

Punishment

The interview asks the interviewee, "What punishment does the perpetrator of the crime deserve?" If the interviewee equivocates, mitigates the criminal's behavior, or suggests a light sentence, then the interviewee is probably not being truthful about his or her innocence.

Process of Elimination

Comments made by witnesses during live line-ups or photograph presentations can indicate the credibility of the identification (Dunning & Stern, 1994). Witnesses who accurately identified suspects in photographic line-ups made statements such as, "His face just popped out at me" (Dunning & Stern, 1994). Witnesses who inaccurately identified suspects in a photographic line-up used the process of elimination to make their identification. Inaccurate witnesses made statements such as, "I compared the photos to each other to narrow the choices" (Dunning & Stern, 1994). This technique is not absolute but merely serves as an indicator for the investigator to make further inquiry of the witness.

Testing an Alibi

Present the interviewee with a conundrum to test his or her alibi (Lieberman, 2000). If the interviewee is telling the truth, the conundrum confirms the interviewee's statement. However, if the interviewee is lying, then he or she must make a decision to either agree with the interviewer or dispute the interviewer's assertion (Lieberman, 2000).

Interviewer: "You said that you were at the Starlight Club all night and could not have committed the crime. I can't find anyone who said that you were there, so I checked the police blotter to see if anything happened that night that you could tell me about, thus verifying that you were at the club. Luckily, for

you, something did happen that night at about the same time the crime was committed. Tell me what happened in the club that night and I'll take you off the prime suspect list. If the interviewee requests more information, make up a fictitious story about a fight that occurred in the club and ask him in what part of the bar the fight occurred. If the interviewee continues to doubt the investigator, the investigator presents the interviewee with a field contact card (prepared by the interviewer prior to the interview) reporting the fictitous fight at the Starlight Club took place at the club's entrance. After this revelation, the interviewee will likely make up a story as to why he could not have possibly seen the fight from where he was sitting in the club. In any event, the conundrum proves the interviewee a liar."

Fabricating False Information

People who fabricate aliases and false addresses, tend to follow certain patterns. Fabricated names are typically derived from the interviewee's relatives, friends, or acquaintances. People also tend to transpose their first and last names when possible. For example, an interviewee will likely change Tracy Lawrence to Lawrence Tracy. People who fabricate addresses tend to change the street number by no more than two numbers. For example, an interviewee will likely change 44335 Foxton Avenue to 335 Foxton Avenue. Street names are often truncated. Apple Orchard Road will likely become Orchard Road. Interviewees will often change street designators such as way, road, lane, court, drive, boulevard. For example, Old Orchard Road will likely become Old Orchard Way. Interviewees will likely change street directional designators. For example, 120 North Clay will likely become 120 South Clay. People rely on these common methods to fabricate names and addresses because, under pressure, these simple changes can appear spontaneous.

Poor Man's Polygraph

Seldom do interviewers have the opportunity to conduct polygraph examinations when conducting routine interviews. The Poor Man's Polygraph is a series of questions that interviewers can ask to increase the probability of detecting deception. These questions are designed to make interviewees think. Liars use most, if not all, of their cognitive processing ability to maintain a lie. Liars have to remember what they said and did not say. They have to control their verbal responses and nonverbal behaviors so as to not to betray the deception. Additionally, liars have to monitor their target's verbal responses and nonverbal behaviors to ensure that the target believes the lie. The mind of a liar is fully occupied, especially if the lie has dire consequences. The goal of the Poor Man's Polygraph is to overload the liar's capacity to think.

When liars are presented with thought-provoking questions, they tend to hesitate to give themselves time to formulate an appropriate answer. If their brains are fully occupied with lying, then there is little thinking capacity to process the new information. Fully occupied brains tend to economize. When liars are presented questions that demand a forced-choice answer they tend to automatically pick one of the choices presented. The questions in the Poor Man's Polygraph are designed to cause cognitive overload or to present forced-choice responses. Truthful people do not experience cognitive overload and, therefore, have enough cognitive processing capacity to easily answer thought-provoking questions. Truthful people also have sufficient cognitive processing to come up with alternative answers when faced with forced-choice questions. The Poor Man's Polygraph is not 100 percent accurate, but it may provide sufficient support to tip the scales toward truth or deception. The Poor Man's Polygraph consists of the following questions and techniques: Why should I believe you?; Parallel Lie; Forced Response; and Well . . . These questions and techniques should not be presented to interviewees in rapid succession, but, rather, the questions should be introduced throughout the interview. This avoids the danger of alerting interviewees to the techniques the interviewers are using.

Why Should I Believe You?

After an interviewee makes a denial, the interviewer should ask, "Why should I believe you?" If the interviewee answers with any variation of the response, "I'm telling the truth," the interviewee is probably telling the truth (Sapir, 1996). The interviewer should make further inquiry if the interviewee provides a different response. Truthful people typically reply, "Because I'm telling the truth" or some derivation thereof. Liars have a difficult time saying, "Because I am telling you the truth" and, instead, offer various other responses. The following exchange between a Customs and Border Patrol (CBP) officer and an airline passenger demonstrates the use of the technique, Why Should I Believe You?

CBP Officer: Did you put the contraband in the suitcase?

Airline Passenger: No, I didn't.

CBP Officer: Sir, believe it or not people lie to CBP Officers. I don't know who you are so why should I believe you?

Airline Passenger: Why would I lie?

CBP Officer: Sir, I didn't ask you why you would lie. I asked you, 'Why I should believe you. Why should I believe you?'

Airline Passenger: I don't know.

CBP Officer: If you don't know why I should believe you then how can I believe you?

Airline Passenger: I guess you don't have too if you don't want to.

At this juncture, the CBP officer indirectly called the airline passenger a liar. When truthful people, are directly or indirectly called liars, they tend to "pushback" by saying something to the effect, "I'm not lying," "I didn't do it," "You're not very good at your job," or "This is ridiculous." Conversely, liars tend to accept the accusation that they are liars with little or no protest. The fact that people do not protest when they are accused of lying does not necessarily mean they are lying, but it does lend support to the hypothesis that the person may be deceptive. Interviewers should only use the response, "I didn't ask you (fill in the blank). I asked you 'Why should I believe you?" no more than three times to avoid the danger of alerting the interviewees to the technique you are using. If the interviewees do not say "Because I am telling you the truth" or some derivation thereof after three tries, then they do not pass this portion of the Poor Man's Polygraph.

Police officers can use this technique on traffic stops. Consider the following example.

Police Officer: Do you have anything in the car that you're not supposed to have?

Driver: No, I don't.

Police Officer: Sir, believe it or not people lie to the police. Why should I believe you?

Driver: Cause I don't do anything I'm not supposed to do?

Police Officer: Sir, I didn't ask you what you did or didn't do. I asked you 'Why should I believe you?

Driver: Sir,... This is crazy... I'm telling you the truth.

Police Officer: And I believe you. Have a nice day.

The driver's answer, ". . . I'm telling you the truth," although it took two tries, suggests that the driver is probably telling the truth. This technique is not a standalone test and should be used in conjunction with other verbal and nonverbal cues to determine the veracity of the driver.

Parallel Lie

The Parallel Lie is the follow-on to the question, "Why should I believe you?" Interviewers do not ask interviewees the same question, but, rather, ask them about the truthfulness of their response to the question. Asking interviewees about the truthfulness of their response adds cognitive load. Since liars are operating at or near full cognitive capacity, they have trouble processing these types of questions and will often hesitate for a moment. When the interviewee hesitates, the interviewer should make the presumptive, "I knew you were lying." or more benign presumptives such as, "I didn't think you were being truthful" or "I thought there was more to the story." Indirectly, interviewers inform interviewees that their stories are not wholly believed. Honest people tend to protest to some degree after being called liars and in many cases display emphatic gestures. Dishonest people tend not to protest after being called liars or become defensive. Observing the interviewee's verbal and nonverbal reaction to the question is more important than the answer itself. Truthful people have little trouble answering a parallel question because they have significant cognitive processing capacity to efficiently process the question. Even if truthful people hesitate, they will usually provide pushback after being called a liar. Again, the Parallel Lie technique does not, in and of itself, indicate deception but it does add support to the hypothesis that the interviewee is being deceptive, especially in conjunction with the question "Why should I believe you?."

 CBP Officer: Sir, remember when you told me that you did not put the contraband in the suitcase, were you telling the truth?

Airline Passenger: Ahh… Yes, I was.

CBP Officer: I knew you lied to me.

Airline Passenger: (Frustrated) I told you the truth. I didn't know you couldn't bring it into the country."

CBP Officer: And I believe you, but I must confiscate the item.

Airline Passenger: No problem. I can do without it.

In this illustration, the airline passenger hesitated and the CBP Officer called the airline passenger a liar. When the airline passenger was called a liar, he provided pushback and said, "I told you the truth . . ." The airline passenger's answer suggests that the he is truthful because he answered with a derivation of "Because I telling you the truth." Even if the airline passenger failed the "Why should I believe you?" question, passing the Parallel Lie supports the hypothesis that the airline passenger is telling the truth.

The following illustration demonstrates the Why should I believe you? Technique along with the Parallel Lie.

 Police Officer: Do you have any drugs in your car?

Driver: No . . . hell no . . . I don't!

Police Officer: Sir, believe it or not people lie to the police. Why should I believe you?

Driver: Cause I don't do drugs?

Police Officer: Sir, I didn't ask you if you do drugs. I asked you 'Why should I believe you?

Driver: Why did you stop me anyway?

Police Officer: Because you were speeding.
Driver: I wasn't going that fast.

Police Officer: Sir, remember when you told me you didn't have any drugs in the car? Were you lying to me?

Driver: Ah . . . .

Police Officer: I knew you lied to me.

Driver: I've got nothing to hide. You can search my car if you want.

Police Officer: I'll take you up on that if you give me permission.

Driver: Go ahead.

The police officer did not ask the driver if drugs were in the car, he asked the driver about his response to the question, "Do you have any drugs in the car?" The driver paused suggesting cognitive overload.

Second Farewell

Sometimes liars let their guard down when they think the interview is over or at the point when they think their interviewers believe the deceptive stories. Officers can take advantage of this psychological phenomenon. The officer could gather up his notes, close his notebook, or put his pen away to give the illusion that the interview is over. As the interviewer starts to leave, the officer calls interviewer back and asks a critical question. Interviewees do not expect additional questioning and may say something incriminating.

The police officer then called the driver a liar. The driver did not protest after the police officer called him a liar. The lack of pushback suggests the driver has drugs in his car. The lack or pushback in conjunction with the failure to correctly answer the question, "Why should I believe you?" adds support to the hypothesis that the driver is deceptive.

Forced Response

The Forced Response can be used as a stand-alone test or it can be used in conjunction with the previous techniques. Liars, when faced with two choices, tend to pick one of the choices presented rather than seeking a third response. This tendency is due to cognitive overload.

When the brain is operating at near-full or full capacity, it tends to economize. Interviewers can take advantage of this phenomenon by asking the question "Do you really want to get away with this?" If the visitor answers, "Yes," the interviewer responds, "That's why I'm here, to stop you from getting away with this." If the visitor answers, "No," the interviewer responds, "That's why I'm here, to stop you from getting away with this." Truthful people will typically respond, "Get away with what?" As with the Parallel Lie technique, the visitor's response to the question is more important than the answer itself. Honest people do answer "Yes" or "No" to the question, but they typically provide pushback when the interviewer indirectly calls them a liar.

Well...

Direct Yes or No questions deserve "Yes" or "No" answers. When interviewees are asked a Yes or No question, and they begin their answer with the word "Well," there is a high probability of deception. Beginning an answer to a direct question with the word "Well" indicates that the interviewee is about to give the interviewer an answer the interviewee knows the interviewer is not expecting. The following exchanges illustrate the Well . . . phenomenon:

Parent: Did you finish your homework?

Child: Well . . .

Parent: Go to your room and finish your homework.

Child: How did you know I didn't do my homework?

Parent: Go do your homework.

The parent need not wait for the child to answer further because the parent knows that the child is going to give an answer the child knows his parent is not expecting. The child knows that the parent is expecting a "Yes" answer to the question, "Did you do your homework?" The child began his response with the word "Well," which means the child is about to give his parent an answer other than "Yes." This technique only works with direct Yes or No questions. Beginning with the word "Well" in response to an open narrative question such as, "Who will win the Super Bowl next year? indicates the person is thinking about how to answer the question. Interviewers should allow interviewees to finish their answers before responding so as not to alert to them to this technique. If interviewees are aware of this technique, they will deliberately avoid using the word "Well."

Consider the following illustration:

Police Officer: Do you know who committed the crime?

Interviewee: Well, I was at the club last night but I didn't see anything out of the ordinary.

Police Officer: I know you know who did it. Let's talk about why you don't want to tell me who did it.

The interviewer asked a direct Yes or No question. The interviewee began her answer with the word "Well," which indicates that the interviewee is about to give the interviewer an answer he knows he is not expecting. The answer the interviewee thinks the interviewer is expecting is "Yes," so the interviewee is about to give the interviewer an answer other than "Yes." The word "Well" suggests that the interviewee knows who committed the crime. The interviewer allowed the interviewee to finish her answer and then used the Presumptive (refer to page 119) to make the interviewee think that the interviewer knows the answer to the question.

The Poor Man's Polygraph does not determine veracity 100 per cent of the time, but it does give interviewers a set of tools to aid in seeking the truth. As with all interviewing techniques, The Poor Man's Polygraph should be used in conjunction with other interviewing techniques.

The Interviewing

Tool Box

The interview proper begins after the interviewer and the intervie- wee establish rapport. If the interviewer encounters little or no resistance from the interviewee, then the requested information flows freely. However, if the interviewer encounters resistance, a wide vari- ety of tools is available to the interviewer. Interviewers must not only learn how to use the tools of persuasion, but they must also learn the limitations of each technique. No one technique works in every inter- view situation; but for every situation there is a technique that will work. Interviewers need multiple techniques in their interviewing repertoire to meet unexpected interview challenges. On average, inves- tigators use six separate techniques during the course of an interview (Leo, 1996).

Pressure

Unlike police interviews portrayed on television, heavy-handed interviewing techniques rarely succeed. Pressure typically fortifies a suspect's resolve not to cooperate (Aronson, 1969; Gudjonsson, 1995).

Patience

The interview process is slow. Obtaining a confession takes time (Inbau, 1999; Szczesny, 2002). Prepare for the long haul. Interviewers should anticipate that a suspect interview will take no less than two hours. Anecdotal evidence suggests that most confessions take over *four hours* to obtain.

Silence

When conversation ceases, people become uncomfortable. The longer the silence endures, the more pressure people feel to fill the void with conversation. Let the interviewee fill the silence.

Set High Expectations

People tend to live up to the expectations of others (Aronson, 1969; Lieberman, 2000). The interviewer should set high expectations for the interviewee at the beginning of the interview. High expectations exert psychological pressure on the interviewee to maintain external and internal consistency.

 Investigator: "You look like an honest person. I expect you to tell the truth."

 Investigator: "You look like a person who admits his mistakes and takes responsibility for his actions."

 Investigator: "You look like a person who does the right thing no matter what happens."

 Investigator: "I admire people who tell the truth. You look like a person of strong moral conviction."

Establish a Pattern of Answering Questions

At the beginning of the interview, get the interviewee into the pattern of answering questions. The interviewer could ask a long series of neutral questions under the premise of gathering personal data and background information. Once the habit is established, the interviewee will more likely answer the more critical questions.

Weight of Evidence Predicts Confession Rate

The strength of the evidence or the suspect's perception of the strength of the evidence is a significant predictor that the suspect will confess (Cassell & Hayman, 1996).

Storytelling

Telling a story evokes emotions and emotions persuade. The interviewer's story should provide a moral and a course of action for the interviewee (Rabon, 1992; McGregor & Holmes, 1999; Strum, 2000; Hicks, 2000).

Interviewer: "This situation reminds me of the time when my sister got in trouble. She was a bank teller. Sometimes, she was a little short of cash and took a few dollars from her cash drawer. She always managed to return the money without getting caught. Over time, she got bolder and took more and more money. One day she got caught. Instead of telling the truth, she lied to cover the missing funds. Her lies became so tangled, she finally told the truth, but it was too late. Instead of just loosing her job, the bank decided to prosecute her because of her dishonesty. My sister didn't call me until it was too late and the charges were already filed; there was nothing I could do for her. If she would have just told the truth in the first place, the worst thing that would have happened is that she would have lost her job. Now look at the trouble she's in, not to mention the possibility of going to jail. Your situation is similar to my sister's situation. You must take responsibility for your actions before things get to the point where I can no longer help you."

Modeling Behavior

Storytelling provides model behavior for the interviewee. The interviewee will likely take the same action if he or she sees that someone else did the right thing when confronted with a similar situation (Sarason, Sarason, Pierce, Shearin, & Sayers, 1991).

Twenty Questions

Some interviewees arrive with myriad questions as to the reason for the interview. The interviewer can capitalize on the interviewee's curiosity by asking him or her, "Why do you think you're here?" The typical response is, "You want to talk to me. How should I know?" The interviewer responds, "Why don't you try to guess why I want to talk to you. You ask me 'yes' or 'no' questions and you'll have 20 questions to figure out why I want to talk to you." The innocent person will not likely play 20 questions because they do not know where to begin the questioning. The guilty person, however, knows very well where to begin the questioning.

(Excerpt from an actual interview)

Suspect: Why am I here?

Detective: Why do you think you're here?

Suspect: I don't know.

Detective: Why don't you try to guess? Ask me yes or no questions. I'll give you twenty tries. It's kinda like the game we played when we were kids.

Suspect: Does it have to do with work?

Detective: Yes. That's one.

Suspect: Does it have to do with my computer at work?

Detective: Yes. That's two.

Suspect: Is it about stuff on my computer that's not supposed to be there?

Detective: Yes. Three.

Suspect: Is it about pornography?

Detective: Yes, but there's more.

Suspect: Child pornography?

Detective: Congratulations . . .

Suspect: I thought so.

Detective: . . . you won the game in five questions. Now tell me how child pornography got on your computer.

Teacher/Student Relationship

In controlled space, the interviewer should equip the interview room with a white board or an easel with paper. At the beginning of the interview or when the interview begins to stall, the interviewer should stand up and present the interviewee and his or her attorney with an overview of the facts surrounding the investigation. The investigator should illustrate on the easel or whiteboard and pause periodically to ask the interviewee and his or her attorney if they understand the points presented by the interviewer. The interviewer, playing the role of the teacher, establishes physical dominance by controlling height and psychological dominance by subordinating the interviewee and his or her attorney to the role of students. At the same time, the interviewer is subconsciously seen as credible.

Confession by a Hundred Admissions

If the interviewee refuses to say the words, "I did the deed," the interviewer can still obtain a confession without the interviewee knowing he or she is confessing. The interviewer should disassemble the crime into its basic components and have the interviewee separately admit to each element.

Probe and Excuse

Bluntly accusing the interviewee of committing a crime or aggressively challenging the interviewee's competence and veracity can be an effective interviewing tool; however, this technique may backfire and anger the interviewee (Gudjonsson, 1995). When this straightforward technique fails, negative feelings can be neutralized if the interviewer provides the interviewee with a simple explanation (Edwards & Potter, 1993; Lieberman, 2000).

Investigator: "You're angry because I asked you some hard questions and pushed things a bit. I'm an investigator. It's my job to ask hard questions. You know you're telling the truth, but I just met you and don't know if you are telling the truth or not. This is a serious matter. I would be remiss as an investigator if I didn't test the veracity of every person I interview. If you were the victim in this case you would expect, no, you would demand that I do everything in my power to solve your case. Now, let's recap your activities on the day the crime occurred."

Ethical Trap

In some instances, a witness possesses guilty knowledge of a crime prior to the apprehension of the offender, or has lied to investigators during a prior interview. The investigator explains to a reluctant witness that he or she fell into an ethical trap, a trap from which few people escape (Schafer, 2002).

When the witness initially became aware of the crime, they chose, for whatever reasons, not to report the crime or to lie to law enforcement officials. Because of their initial decision not to report the crime or to lie, the witness now faces a larger decision with more severe consequences: prosecution for aiding and abetting a crime after the fact, or an administrative action resulting in the loss of his or her job.

The witness faces this dilemma: if I tell the truth now, I must explain why I didn't come forward when I first became aware of the crime, or if I lie now to cover my initial lie, the possibility exists that I might face legal and/or administrative sanctions. The ethical trap puts the witness in a lose/lose position, which obviates the witness' initial reluctance to report. The interviewer offers the interviewee the only way out: Do the morally correct thing now and tell the truth.

Fill in the Dots

The brain fills in the blanks. A children's dot-to-dot book illustrates this phenomenon. The adult brain connects the dots and correctly identifies the figure without physically connecting the dots with a pencil. Investigators can take advantage of this phenomenon by mentally and physically presenting the available evidence to the interviewee in a pattern that suggests the interviewer knows all the facts in the case. Even though the nexus between the evidence and the interviewee is weak or perhaps nonexistent, the guilty person's brain will automatically fill in the gaps and assume the interviewer knows the full story, making a confession more likely.

Presumptive

The investigator enters the interview with the presumption that he or she already knows the interviewee is guilty. The interviewer rejects all notions of innocence by the interviewee. The interviewer seeks only reasons why the interviewee committed the crime. The success of the presumptive interview relies on the existence of evidence or strong circumstantial evidence suggesting the interviewee committed the crime.

Accepting Possibilities

If the interviewee will not admit to any wrongdoing, then get him or her to admit to possibilities. Getting the interviewee to admit to the possibility of an action moves the interviewee one step closer to a confession.

 Interviewer: "I know you said you don't know how the child pornography got onto your work computer. The fact remains your computer contains child pornography. We both agree it had to get there somehow. I know you wouldn't do it intentionally. Is it possible you accidentally downloaded the child pornography when you were downloading other files?"

 Interviewer: "Is it possible that you were on the Internet and accessed a pornography site without realizing it?"

 Interviewer: "Is it possible that when you saw the pornography site, it took you a few minutes to realize what it was before you left the site?"

 Interviewer: "Is it possible that you received an email advertising a pornography site and clicked on the site out of curiosity? Pornography distributors send mass emails hoping curiosity will ensnare someone."

You Choose

The interviewer presents the interviewee with two diametrically opposed options. The interviewer places the interviewee in a no-win position. In the example above, the interviewee must choose between admitting that he or she accidentally downloaded pornography or admit to being a child molester. The interviewee will likely deny being a child molester and admit to the possibility that the he or she accidentally downloaded child pornography or viewed it out of curiosity.

Investigator: "There is a big difference between accidentally accessing a pornography site and intentionally seeking it out. Either you accidentally downloaded child pornography or you're a child molester. Those are the only choices. You choose. Are you a curiosity seeker or are you a child molester?"

Eighteen-Year Rookie

Rookies have one big advantage. They can ask questions, lots of very basic questions. Interviewees are less likely to become impatient or angry because he or she is just a rookie and rookies aren't supposed to know much. If the interviewer does not command the topic of the interview, he or she should inform the interviewee of this fact. By so doing, the interviewer does not have to pretend to be an expert on the interview topic and has the freedom to ask as many questions, including stupid questions, as needed to obtain information from the interviewee. If he interviewee balks, the interviewer simply says, "I'm a rookie at this, maybe you could teach me a few things." An experienced interviewer can get away with asking very probing questions under the guise of being a rookie.

Teach Me

This technique works well in complicated investigations requiring multiple interviews. An interviewee with guilty knowledge will inevitably tell the interviewer that due to the complex nature of the inquiry, the investigator does not understand the nature of the case. Instead of pretending to possess as much knowledge as the interviewee, the interviewer should simply ask the interviewee to teach the interviewer the process. At the end of the first interview, the interviewer should ask the interviewee if he or she would serve as the interviewer's consultant in the investigation. This technique ostensibly empowers the interviewee to direct the investigation and gives the interviewer unlimited access to the interviewee to solicit information and build rapport.

Once the interviewer gains sufficient knowledge, he or she can confront the interviewee with the truth and secure a confession.

Micro-Action Interview

Text Bridges locate withheld information. If the interviewer deems the withheld information important, a Micro-action Interview closes the information gap by a systematic accounting of all the interviewee's time and behaviors during the information gap. Interviewers can use the Micro-action Interview to extract more detailed information from interviewees and reveal deception in both social and professional settings. The Micro-action Interview differs from other interviewing techniques in that interviewers ask the simple question, "What happened next?" Innocent people convey information; guilty people put themselves in the psychological vise.

The systematic narrowing of the information gap acts like a psychological vise. The unique feature of the Micro-action Interview is that innocent people do not experience stress because they are telling the truth; guilty people place themselves in a self-tightening psychological vise. As the information gap closes, deceptive interviewees experience more stress because they are continually seeking ways to circumvent the withheld information. As the self-induced stress increases, interviewees engage their own flight-fight response. The associated nonverbal cues serve as a gauge for veracity. Truthful people will not display the nonverbal indicators of deception as the information gap closes. Truthful people may complain about having to answer so many questions, but will answer them because they have nothing to hide.

The Micro-action Interview begins at the point just before the Text Bridge. The interviewer should anchor the interviewee. Anchoring simply means having the interviewee describe his or her position just prior to the Text Bridge. After anchoring the interviewee, the interviewer should ask the simple question "What happened next?" The interviewee will typically provide additional information and use another Text Bridge to circumvent the withheld information. The interviewer should go back to just before the second Text Bridge, anchor the interviewee and ask, "What happened next?" The interviewer should continue this process until the information gap closes or until the interviewee shows signs of deception. If deception is indicated, the interviewer should continue closing the information gap or use alternate interviewing techniques.

Repeatedly asking the question, "What happened next?" can detract from the interview, so investigators should intersperse self-deprecating remarks such as: "I'm sorry. I zoned out for a second. Let's go back to (the point just prior to the last Text Bridge);" "My brain is not processing as fast as you are talking, can we back up to (the point just prior to the last Text Bridge)?;" or "I'm confused; you said you were (refer to the action just prior to the last Text Bridge).

The following excerpt from a transcript of an interview between an accident investigator and a driver demonstrates the application of the Micro-action Interview. The Micro-action Interview forced the driver to reveal the real cause of the accident.

Investigator: Describe what happened.

Driver: I looked up, saw the car coming toward me, and then I tried to avoid hitting the car.

(The words *looked up* indicate that the driver was not looking at the road when the accident happened.)

Investigator: You saw the car coming toward you. What happened next?

Investigator: I put both hands on the wheel and then tried to avoid hitting the car.

(The words *both hands* indicate that the driver did not have both hands on the wheel when the accident occurred.)

Investigator: Let's back up. You put both your hands on the wheel. What happened next?

Driver: I put my foot on the brake and then the car went out of control.

Investigator: I'm sorry. I must have missed something. You put your foot on the brake. What happened next?

Driver: The brake didn't work and then I pushed.

Investigator: I'm a little confused. You pushed harder on the brake but the car didn't slow down. What happened next?

Driver: I tried to kick the cell phone out of the way. It must have fallen down when I grabbed the wheel.

Investigator: So, you were talking on your cell phone when the accident occurred.

(Based on the information gained from the Micro-action Interview in conjunction with other verbal indicators, the investigator tested his hypothesis using a presumptive statement.)

Driver: Yeah.

Investigator: You dropped your cell phone, tried to retrieve it, and lost control of the car?

(The investigator followed the driver's admission with a follow-up presumptive statement.)

Driver: I just took my eyes off the road for a second. I thought it was safe to pick up my phone.

Pencils Have Erasers

The interviewer concedes to the interviewee that all people make mistakes. The interviewer further tells the interviewee that pencils have erasers for that very reason. The interviewer concludes that the eraser can take the black mark off the paper but the indentation the pencil made is still there and that's what must be dealt with. The interviewer then proposes that it's up to the interviewee to choose between dealing with the black mark as well as the indentation in the paper or erase the black mark and just deal with the indentation. The interviewee is put in a position that gives the illusion that he or she is in charge of his or her own destiny. This technique also lets the interviewee know that no matter what option he or she chooses, there will be consequences.

Now or Never

Whenever the interviewer presents the interviewee with a proposition, a deadline should be attached (Lieberman, 2000). Deadlines lend a sense of urgency. The interviewer should increase his or her speech cadence to add a sense of urgency to the situation.

Interviewer: "You have to make a decision about whether or not you are going to cooperate before you leave the room today."

Us Against Them

The interviewer should try to set up a scenario pitting the interviewer and the interviewee (us) against the government, supervisors, or administrators (them). The interviewer and the interviewee are now on the same side coordinating their efforts against a nebulous "them." The "I" becomes" we."

Get the Interviewee to Request a Polygraph Examination

The interviewee may balk if the interviewer suggests a polygraph examination; therefore, the interviewer should provide a scenario wherein the logical solution is a polygraph examination. Under these conditions, the interviewee is likely to suggest that he or she take a polygraph examination to resolve the matter.

(The polygraph test has been prearranged and the polygrapher is standing by in a nearby room.)

Interviewer: Well, I'm out of ideas. (The interviewer shrugs his or her shoulders and leans back). My supervisor will never let me close this case simply because you said you didn't do it. If you say you didn't do it, I believe you, but look at the evidence. If there were only some way we could objectively show my supervisor that you didn't do it. What would you do if you were me?

Interviewee: I don't know.

Interviewer: There must be some way. Let's think. (Pause) We need to find something objective that my supervisor can't refute.

(The interviewer and interviewee exchange a few ideas but the interviewer always finds an excuse why the interviewee's suggestion won't work until. . . .)

Interviewee: How about a polygraph test?

Interviewer: That's a good idea, but I don't think I can get it set up for a few weeks and I don't want to keep you hanging that long. Let's think of another way.

Interviewee: A polygraph is objective.

Interviewer: Yeah, and my supervisor will let me close the case if you pass, which I have no doubt that you will. (pause) I've got it. A friend of mine is a polygrapher. He owes me a favor. Let me call him and see what I can do.

(The interviewer picks up the phone and calls the polygrapher within earshot of the interviewee)

Interviewer: Hi, this is (interviewer). Are you busy right now?

Polygrapher: (Not heard)

Interviewer: Good. Let me ask you a favor. Can you do a polygraph test for me today?

Polygrapher: (Not heard)

Interviewer: I know it's short notice. You owe me for the time I helped you last month.

Polygrapher: (Not heard)

Interviewer: It won't take long. The guy didn't do it.

Polygrapher: (Not heard)

Interviewer: What are friends for if you can't take advantage of them? Thanks. We'll be right over.

(The interviewer hangs up the phone)

Interviewer: We're in luck. There was a cancellation. If we go right now, the polygrapher can do it. Boy, you're lucky. This polygrapher is very competent. He's fair, open-minded, and listens to people. This polygrapher can just look at a person and tell if they're lying. Let's go.

Interviewee: Thanks for helping me.

Interviewer: I'd do anything to help a friend who tells the truth.

Everybody Makes Mistakes

Tell the interviewee that he or she acted out of ignorance not intent. The interviewer should emphasize the difference between a good person who makes a mistake and a bad person who commits a crime.

Interviewer: "Everybody makes mistakes. That's why all my pencils have erasers."

Interviewer: "You made a mistake. So what, take responsibility and get on with your life."

Persuade–Don't Negotiate

By definition, negotiations are adversarial. The premise of negotiations supposes that both sides must give something up to get something from one another (Aubuchon, 1997). Negotiating assumes a winner and a loser and no one wants to be a loser. Persuasion is the process whereby the interviewer guides the interviewee through the decision-making process. Gaining a confession through the power of persuasion maintains the illusion that the interviewee controls his or her destiny.

Created Power

Final decision-makers possess real power. The interviewer possesses real power in that he or she makes final decisions in an interview. Created power provides the illusion that the less powerful possess a greater degree of real power. The interviewer can confer power as easily as he or she can withdraw power. The interviewer bestows created power to an otherwise powerless interviewee, meets the interview objective, and then withdraws the created power, leaving the interviewee bewildered.

This technique works best when the interviewee possesses superior knowledge or displays narcissistic or psychopathic personality traits. Created power gives the interviewee a false sense of superiority over the interviewer. This false sense of security leads to a false sense of confidence that the interviewee can out-smart the interviewer and escape detection. This false sense of confidence provides a motive for the interviewee to engage the interviewer in multiple interviews.

The major obstacle to the successful use of this technique is the interviewer's own ego. During the portion of the interview when the interviewee exercises created power, the interviewer must appear subservient and likely endure subtle slights and perhaps direct insults from the interviewee. This technique appears to give the interviewee control of the interview; however, this is not the case. The interviewer maintains full control of the interview in that he or she holds final decision-making authority even when the interviewee believes the opposite is true.

Implicit Communication

When people read or listen to others, they tend to read between the lines (Kassin, 1997). Based on this tendency, investigators can explicitly communicate with the suspect. When an investigator talks to a suspect about a maximum sentence, this statement suggests a harsh outcome, and when an investigator talks about a minimum sentence, this statement suggests leniency.

Tell a Secret

The interviewee will feel obligated to tell the interviewer a secret if the interviewer tells a secret to the interviewee (Collins & Miller, 1994). Research on self-disclosure and attraction divides into two categories, disclosure as a social exchange and disclosure as a derivation of positive attraction (Collins & Miller, 1994).

Disclosure functions as a measure of social relationships. The more intense the exchange, the closer the social relationship becomes. Self-disclosure signals the willingness of one person to initiate a closer relationship with another person, which positively predisposes the recipient of the secret information to like the person who disclosed the secret. The recipient of the secret receives a social reward, which reinforces reciprocal behavior (Collins & Miller, 1994; Dalto, Ajzen, & Kaplan, 1979; Dimitrius & Mazzarella, 2000). People form positive impressions of people who disclose intimate information (Davis &

Sloan, 1974; Jones & Archer, 1976; Kleinke & Kahn, 1980). Additionally, people who disclose intimate information are seen as more trusting, friendly, and warmer than people who are not as forthcoming (Ajzen, 1977).

 Investigator: "I never told anyone this before, but your case reminds me of something I did when I was a kid. I was supposed to save my allowance for a new bike. Each week my mother put my allowance in a piggy bank and told me that by the end of the year I would have enough money to buy a new bike. I kept taking the money out to buy candy and other kid stuff. I mowed lawns and shoveled snow so I could get enough money to replace the money I took out of the piggy bank. The more money I took, the more lawns I had to mow. Right before I was suppose to buy the bike, the piggy bank was short about five dollars. It was winter so I prayed for snow, but no snow came. I know the stress you are going through. When you start taking money from the cash drawer with the intent of replacing it later, the vicious cycle begins. Unfortunately, some people get caught before they can replace the money."

The Ambush

During a lull in the interview, when you are casually discussing a nonspecific topic, suddenly look the interviewee directly in the eye and sternly ask, "Did you (fill in the crime)?" The abrupt change from a friendly countenance to a sterner tone in conjunction with a critical question may provoke the suspect to inadvertently display deceptive indicators.

When It Rains, It Pours

The interviewer tells the interviewee that it is obvious that he or she committed the crime; all the evidence points toward the interviewee.

The interviewer then draws the following analogy: If you wake up to a sunny morning but the streets, the ground, and the rooftops are wet, you know it rained even though you didn't see or hear the storm the previous night. I may not have seen you commit the crime, but all the evidence tells me you did. It's too late to pull out your umbrella, you're already soaking wet.

Reinterview

In the event the interviewer cannot determine if the suspect is telling the truth or lying, a second interview should be conducted to compare inconsistencies in the two interviews. Comparing statement inconsistencies is the most common method used by investigators to detect deception (Granhag & Stromwall, 2001; Granhag & Stromwall, 2000).

Multiple Interviews

Not all suspects are candidates for a multiple interview strategy. Multiple interviews are helpful when interviewing witnesses or suspects during long, complicated investigations. Multiple interviews are also helpful when interviewing suspects displaying complex personalities. The primary objectives of the first interview are to establish rapport with the suspect, to present a nonthreatening environment, and to gather as much personal information in preparation for subsequent interviews.

Multiple interviews can be more effective if the interviewer(s) carefully script each interview and establish specific written goals. At the conclusion of each interview, the interviewer(s) should determine which objectives were accomplished and which objectives were not. Based on information obtained from the first interview, the interviewer(s) should set specific goals for the second interview. Each interview should incrementally propel the investigation toward a resolution. Multiple interviews are doomed to failure if they are not carefully planned.

With all multiple interview scenarios, the primary question is, "Will the suspect actually come to a second interview without consulting an attorney?" The answer is usually "yes," but the investigator must give the suspect a compelling explicit or implicit reason to return. Each suspect has a different motivation; therefore, the investigator(s) must craft a reason to return based on the suspect's personality and life circumstances.

The following example illustrates the use of multiple interviews of a psychopath.

The first interview was conducted in the suspect's home. This venue was chosen because people feel comfortable at home and in control of the interview theater. Upon arrival at the suspect's home, the investigators displayed submissive gestures such as downward eye gazes, palms up handshake presentations, indirect eye contact during conversation, soft vocal intonations, and allowed the suspect to sit in an elevated position. In short, the suspect totally controlled and dominated the interview and the interviewers. In fact, when the suspect's wife arrived home, she asked how things were going. The suspect replied, "I'm having great fun playing with these investigators." The investigators nodded and smiled sheepishly.

The first interview yielded a wealth of information about the suspect's personality, method of domination, and lifestyle. Equally important, the suspect became overly confident that he could control the investigators and talk his way out of his predicament, thus significantly increasing the probability of a second interview.

The second interview was conducted in an interview room at the police station furnished with only three chairs. The investigators greeted the suspect with dominant handshake presentations, stern voices, and kept the suspect focused. The investigators systematically presented the evidence and asked the suspect to choose one of the options offered. The suspect provided a partial confession and agreed to a third interview on the following day.

The third interview was conducted in the same interview room. During this interview, the suspect complimented the investigators on their "slick" interviewing skills. The suspect commented that he realized that he had been "played" when he shook hands with the interviewers at the beginning of the second interview. The suspect considered the interviewers as equals and consequently provided a full confession.

Inoculation

A drawback to multiple interviews is the fact that interviewees become familiar with the interviewer's tactics and can more easily read the interviewer's verbal and nonverbal behaviors, thus becoming "inoculated" (Navarro, 2000). Consequently, the interviewer is rendered less effective and more susceptible to manipulation by the interviewee. Also, investigators who conduct multiple interviews of the same suspect tend to judge the suspect as truthful because, over time, the subject's verbal and nonverbal behaviors tend to mimic the verbal and nonverbal behaviors of an honest person (Granhag & Stromwall, 2001; Burgoon et al., 1999).

The Anger Cycle

Chapter

12

During interviews, interviewees may become angry. Anger stems from varied sources such as getting caught, loss of control, or the betrayal of a codefendant. No matter what the source of the anger, it must be dealt with before the interview can continue. One of the cardinal rules of interviewing is "Do not engage angry people." Control the anger first and then proceed toward the interview objective. When the interviewer engages an angry interviewee, they get caught in the anger cycle. The anger cycle works like this: the interviewee makes an angry statement to the interviewer; the interviewer responds in kind stoking the interviewee's anger, the interviewee, feeding off the interviewer's response becomes angrier and makes another angry statement, which, in turn, prompts another angry response from the interviewer. The anger cycle will continue as long as the interviewer adds fresh fuel to heighten the interviewee's anger. Anger control techniques prevent verbal conflicts from escalating and can calm angry interviewees.

Recognizing the absence or deterioration of rapport is the first step to controlling anger. Interviewers should continually monitor the interviewee's verbal and nonverbal cues that signal increasing or decreasing rapport. If rapport decreases, interviewers can use several techniques to either increase rapport or, in extreme cases, to control anger or the possibility of verbal escalation.

Provide an Explanation

Anger tends to dissipate when interviewers provide an explanation for their actions. Once the interviewee understands why the interviewer acted as he or she did, mild anger tends to dissipate.

Suspect: Why did you put handcuffs on me in front of my wife and kids? You just did that to humiliate me.

Interviewer: Sir, I put handcuffs on you because it is department policy that whenever an officer arrests someone, they must be handcuffed when being transported to the police station. The primary reason for handcuffs is for officer safety.

Suspect: I guess you were just doing your job.

Breaking the Anger Cycle

If the interviewee does not accept the explanation and verbally escalates the conversation, the interviewer should break the anger cycle before continuing the interview. Breaking the anger cycle controls anger and allows the interviewee to safely vent his or her anger and redirects them toward the interview objective.

The first step in breaking the anger cycle is to construct an empathic statement. In addition to rapport building, empathic statements control anger. Confronting anger with anger or officious statements will not stem the interviewee's anger but, instead, will likely intensify the anger. The interviewer should wait for a natural break in the interviewer's initial complaint and then respond with an empathic statement. After making an empathic statement, the interviewer should expect venting.

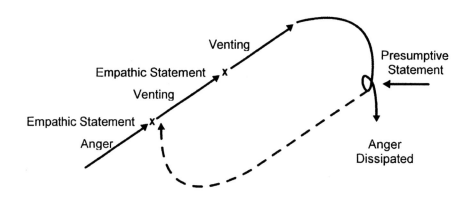

Venting allows the angry interviewee to more fully express his or her anger. The interviewer should wait for a natural break in the interviewer's venting and then respond with a second empathic statement. After making the empathic statement, the interviewer should again expect additional venting, although it will probably be less intense. The interviewer should continue this process until the interviewee's anger diminishes. Sighs, long exhales, slumping shoulders, downward glances signal spent anger. At this juncture, interviewers should introduce a presumptive statement.

Presumptive Statement

The presumptive statement creates the illusion that the interviewee has control over his or her actions. In reality, the presumptive statement forces the interviewee to take a predetermined course of action and directs the angry interviewee into a position of acquiesce. If an angry interviewee rejects the presumptive statement, the interviewer should begin the anger cycle again with an empathic statement.

The following example illustrates how to break the anger cycle.

Suspect: Why did you put handcuffs on me in front of my wife and kids? You just did that to humiliate me.

Interviewer: Sir, I put handcuffs on you because it is department policy that whenever an officer arrests someone, they must be handcuffed when being transported to the police station. The primary reason for handcuffs is for officer safety.

Suspect: You humiliated me in front of my family. That's just wrong. All you cops think you're so high and mighty and you can do anything you want.

(Providing an explanation did not work, so the interviewer introduces breaking the anger cycle technique.)

Interviewer: So you were embarrassed when I put handcuffs on you in front of your family. (Empathic statement)

Suspect: I'm not a threat to anyone. You have the gun I don't. You're just drunk with power. You had to make me look small in front of my family to make yourself look good. (venting)

Interviewer: So you think your family will think less of you because you were arrested (Empathic statement.)

Interviewee: I didn't do anything wrong. This is all a big mistake.

Interviewer: So you think I made a big mistake arresting you. (Empathic statement.)

Interviewee: Yeah, I'm innocent. (sigh) (Spent anger)

Interviewer: Let's work together to sort this thing out. So you can get back to your family as soon as possible. Would you like that? (Presumptive statement.)

Interviewee: Yeah, I would.

Interviewer: Good. I have a few questions to ask you. Let's get started. (Redirection toward the interview objective.)

The presumptive statement forces the interviewee into a position where he or she has to say "Yes" or appear insincere. If the interviewee does continue to make angry statements, the interviewer re-enters the angry cycle.

Re-entering the Anger Cycle

In the event the interviewee remains angry and does not calm down, the interviewer re-enters the anger cycle by making another empathic statement. The following is a continuation of the previous exchange.

Interviewer: Let's work together to sort this thing out. So you can get back to your family as soon as possible. Would you like that? (Presumptive statement.)

Interviewee: No, I wouldn't. I want you to do your job and not come into innocent people's houses and humiliate them in front of their families. (The interviewee does not agree with the presumptive statement.)

Interviewer: So you're upset because the police came to your house and arrested you in front of your family. (The interviewer reenters the anger cycler with an empathic statement.)

The interviewer would continue going through the anger cycle until the interviewee's anger is spent. The interviewer could periodically use the presumptive statement to gage the intensity of the interviewee's anger. Since empathic statements mirror the angry person's feelings back to them using parallel language, the interviewer does not add fuel to the interviewee's anger. Eventually, the interviewee's anger subsides. Once the interviewee calms down, the interviewer can redirect the focus of the interview toward the interview objective.

Stealth Mode

To a person who is not angry, the repeated use of the empathic statement may appear patronizing, which, in turn, causes the angry interviewee to become even angrier. This is not the case. When a person becomes angry, the fight/flight reaction engages causing emotional flooding. Angry people react to what is said without thinking. During emotional flooding, the angry person automatically responds. Emotional flooding allows interviewers to effectively guide interviewees through the anger cycle with little probability of detection.

You Choose

In the event re-entering the anger cycle does not calm the intervie-wee, the interviewer should develop two options and allow the inter-viewee to choose one of the options. Giving the interviewee two options creates the illusion that the interviewee is in control. In reality, either option redirects the interviewee toward the interview objective. Forcing the interviewee to choose his or her course of action allows the interviewer to neutralize future objections by the interviewee. The interviewer responds to the interviewee's objections by saying, "I gave you a choice and you chose this course of action. You are the one caus-ing yourself additional trouble not me." The You Choose technique holds the interviewee responsible for his or her own actions.

The following exchange, an extension of the previous exchange, illustrates the You Choose technique.

Interviewer: We could sit here and banter back and forth, which would prolong the resolution of this sit-uation and keep you away from your family longer or we could get down to business, prove your innocence and return home as quickly as possible. The choice is yours. You'll have to make a decision.

If the interviewee is reluctant to make a decision or does not want to choose either of the options, the interviewer should question the inter-viewee's premise.

Investigator: So, being with your family is not really the reason that you're upset.

Questioning the interviewee's premise forces him or her to choose one of the two options presented or abandon the premise and offer another excuse why he or she does not want to cooperate with the interviewer. When faced with this possibility, interviewees typically choose one of the options. No matter which option the interviewee selects, the interviewer moves the interview towards the interview objective.

In each of these scenarios, the interviewer maintained the illusion that the interviewee was in control of the situation, but, in reality, the interviewer directed the interviewee one step at a time toward the interview objective.

Aggressive Probing

Breaking the anger cycle can also be used in conjunction with Aggressive Probing. When an interviewee reacts angrily to a probing question, the interviewer could guide the visitor through the anger cycle to calm him or her down. Once the interviewee is calm, the interviewer reestablishes rapport and then can ask additional probing questions. The technique of breaking the anger cycle, build rapport, and asking probing questions allow interviewers to maintain control, while, at the same time, aggressively probe noncompliant interviewees.

Breaking the Impasse and Other Problems

The interviewer serves as a facilitator to set and maintain the optimum pace of the interview. If the information is flowing smoothly, the interviewer should not interrupt the interview process. However, if the interview stalls, the interviewer and the interviewee are at an impasse, the most critical point in an interview. The interviewee will not confess and the interviewer does not know what to do.

Confronting Resistance

If the interviewee shows stiff resistance and is reluctant to continue the interview, the interviewer should stop the current line of questioning, acknowledge the interviewee's unwillingness to tell the truth, and confront the interviewee's reasons for not telling the truth.

Investigator: "I get the feeling that you really don't want to talk about this. Let's put the interview aside and talk about how you feel." Allow the interviewee to express his or her feelings about the interview. The interviewer can stimulate conversation by asking the following questions: "Do you feel that you're being treated unfairly?" "Are you afraid of going to jail." "Do you feel like you're being accused of something you didn't do?" "Tell me what's between you and the truth."

Pick a Number–Any Number

Ask the interviewee to pick a number between one and one million and instruct him or her to write the number on a piece of paper without revealing it (Lieberman, 2000). The interviewer then makes the following proposition, "If I can guess the number you just wrote down, will you tell me the truth?" If the interviewee replies, "Yes," it signals the interviewee's willingness to continue talking (Lieberman, 2000). If the interviewee replies, "no," it signals the interviewee's lack of willingness to continue the interview and the interviewer should change to a different interview strategy. Both "yes" and "no" answers signal the truth has yet to be revealed.

Feelings vs. Facts

Humans make decisions based on their emotions rather than facts. Shifting the focus of the interview from facts to feelings overcomes resistance.

Up the Proverbial Waterway

The interviewer reviews the evidence with the interviewee using courtroom symbology and offers the interviewee the only obvious solution–tell the truth.

Interviewer: "Let's take a minute here to review the facts. I know you said you didn't do it, but let's just pretend that you are one of 12 objective people off the street. (The interviewer begins) Ladies and gentlemen of the jury let me present the evidence (the interviewer reviews the evidence against the interviewee). Now, after hearing all the evidence, how say you? Without your side of the story (interviewee's name), your life will change from this day forward. The facts are certain. If I were one of those 12 people, your motive would make all the difference between a guilty or not guilty verdict. I'm giving you that chance right

now. Tell me what really happened and why you did what you did."

The Sleep of the Righteous

The interviewer tells the interviewee that he or she is spending so much time with the interviewee not because the interviewer wants to help the interviewee, but because the interviewer wants to soothe his or her own conscience. If, in fact, the interviewee is innocent, as he or she so vehemently claims in spite of the overwhelming evidence to the contrary, the interviewer needs to make sure that the interviewee has every opportunity to tell the truth, because the interviewer does not want to lose sleep thinking an innocent person went to prison.

Get Up and Go

The interviewer tells the interviewee that it's obvious that he or she does not want help. So why should the interviewer try to help someone who doesn't want to help themselves. The interviewer then firmly tells the interviewee to get up and go if he doesn't want the interviewer's help. If the interviewee hesitates, the interviewer should point to the door and firmly say, "Get up and go." The guilty person will not leave in a more agitated emotional state than when he or she arrived. The interviewee should be left in silence for a short period. The interviewer should then say, "Tell me the truth so I can help you." In the event the interviewee does start to get up, the interviewer should ask, "Do you want to know what's going to happen next?" The guilty person will likely re-engage the interviewer.

Do You Feel Lucky?

The interviewer tells the interviewee that it's obvious that he or she is not going to tell the truth nor can the interviewer force the interviewee to tell the truth. The interviewer tells the interviewee that only he or she knows if he or she committed the crime; the interviewer can only speculate, since all the facts are not yet known. The interviewer then tells the interviewee that he or she must decide if the interviewer (you) is smart enough to uncover the evidence needed to arrest the interviewee. For example:

Detective: It's obvious that you don't want to tell me the truth.

Suspect: Yeah.

Detective: You also know that I can't make you tell the truth.

Suspect: You got that right.

Detective: You are going to have to make a decision. You know what you did. I can only speculate. I don't have all the evidence and I'll tell you that straight up. Now you must gamble that I don't have the skills to get the evidence. If you cooperate and take responsibility now, the prosecutor and the judge will take that into consideration. When I find the evidence without your help, then it's too late. Look into my eyes. I'm a bulldog. I'll make you my hobby case. Instead of chatting at the office cooler, I'll be investigating this case. You're taking a big gamble. Do you feel lucky? I wouldn't be feeling very lucky if I were you. I think you should tell me the truth now and save yourself a lot more trouble later.

Your Only Chance to Tell Your Side

The interviewer tells the interviewee that this might be the only chance to tell his or her side of the story. The interviewer reviews the evidence and tells the interviewee, "I'd be happy to go to court with these facts because they make you look guilty. It's up to you. If you want me to write the story, I'll include all the facts I just showed you, which won't make you look very good. Now may be the only opportunity you have outside the courtroom to not only tell your side of the story in your own words but to explain why you did it. The choice is yours. I know what I'd do if I were you."

Force Movement

Forcing an interviewee to change his or her physical position often will lead to a change in a person's mental position (Lieberman, 1998).

Saving Face

Themes can be developed which can help the interviewee save face and help him or her overcome psychological hurdles, allowing him or her to make an admission or even a confession (Gregory, 1999). Some of these themes are:

- Your employer victimized you.
- Your talents were not recognized.
- You did not get sufficient credit for your hard work.
- No one ever understood all your good qualities.
- You did not receive the promotions and/or preferred assignments you deserved .
- They treated you as an outsider, not as one of the "good 'ol boys."
- Your employer/boss never supported you or your ideas.

Reasons for Cooperating

- As of today, your life has changed. There is no going back.
- Out of respect and in fairness to you, we have come to you first.
- It's your chance to have control over what happens next.
- It's your chance to tell your side of the story.
- Today, it's in your hands.
- We will be required to write a report based on this conversation. It will go to influential people. What should we write?
- Your knowledge is the only "currency" you have. You might want to "spend" some now.
- Take responsibility now. Act honorably for yourself and your family.
- You can stop looking over your shoulder.
- You will feel relief after unburdening yourself.

- Good people make mistakes. They can ask for forgiveness.
- Do the right and/or smart thing.
- We will keep this as private as possible. Family, friends, colleagues, neighbors, church, and the media need not know unless you want them to know.
- Absent your help, we will be forced to intensify the investigation. This will include interviews of all of your neighbors, friends, family, and so forth. What do you want us to tell them? (Gregory, 1999)

Hard Questions

A good investigator will have ready answers to the following questions, which may pose a challenge for the unprepared investigator (Gregory, 1999).

- Am I under arrest?
- Do you intend to arrest me?
- Perhaps I should listen to what you have to say and I should just be quiet?
- How much trouble am I in?
- Do I need a lawyer?
- Am I free to go?
- What evidence do you have?
- Who else knows about this case?
- How long have you known?
- Have you been following me?
- Does my family or spouse know about this?
- What happens next?
- How many years will I have to serve?
- What if I resign today?
- What can you do for me if I cooperate?
- What's the incentive for me to cooperate?
- Can I get amnesty if I cooperate?
- Will I go to prison?
- What about my spouse and kids?
- Does anyone else have to know?
- Will this be in all the newspapers?
- What kind of prison will I be sent to?

- Will I be under surveillance after this interview?
- What should I do?
- Can I talk to my wife briefly?
- Can I talk to my priest before I answer?
- Can I ask my best friend what to do at this point?

The End Game

The end of an interview is just as important as the beginning of the interview. If done properly, the interviewee will be more receptive to a second interview. The end of the interview is a time for both the interviewer and interviewee to decompress and resolve any outstanding issues. Time to undo the interview knot.

Thank the Interviewee/Suspect

Interviewers should thank interviewees for their cooperation and reassure them that they did the right thing by cooperating.

Resolve Dissonance

Dissonance occurs when people hold two diametrically opposed ideas about themselves (Festinger, 1957; Aronson, 1969). Dissonance is an uncomfortable condition and people seek to reduce it by changing the emotional or physical conditions in their lives in an attempt to reconcile the differences (Aronson, 1969). Dissonance usually occurs when people confess to crimes that are out of character. A president of a business or a community leader will have a more difficult time admitting that he or she has committed a crime. Hardened criminals, on the other hand, experience less dissonance because their self-image is consistent with their actions. Dissonance can be resolved by providing rationalizations for the interviewee's actions.

Provide Hope

People who confess to a crime may lose hope and feel as though their world has collapsed around them and that suicide is the only option left. The investigator should provide the interviewees with hope by discussing the possibility of a normal life once the matter at hand is resolved.

Investigator: "You did the right thing. Taking responsibility for your actions is the first step in the healing process. Once this is resolved, you can pick up your life right where you left off. Everything is going to be okay."

Recontact

The investigator should provide the interviewee a means for recontact. In many instances, witnesses and even suspects will recontact the investigator and provide additional information or a confession.

After an initial unsuccessful interview of a murder suspect, the investigator concluded the interview on a positive note and provided the suspect with a business card. Two months later, the suspect recontacted the investigator and provided a full confession. The investigator asked the suspect what motivated him to recontact the investigator. The suspect replied, "I like you because you were the only person who treated me with respect and listened to me."

Escort the Interviewee to the Exit

No matter what the outcome of the interview, the interviewer should shake hands with the interviewee and escort him or her out to the exit door of the building, if possible, and not just to office door. This will leave a lasting impression on the interviewee and encourage future contact and thus, increase the possibility that the interviewee will provide information concerning the inquiry or any future information regarding other criminal violations.

The Interview Postmortem

After the interview, investigators should always perform an interview postmortem. They should ask themselves, "What went wrong?" "What went right?" and "What could they have done differently to make the interview more effective?" Evaluate the effectiveness of any new techniques that may have been tried. If a new technique did not work as well as anticipated, discuss how to change the technique to make it more effective. Be honest with yourselves. Making mistakes is part of the learning process and the lessons learned should be incorporated into future interviews.

Remember, interviewing is the most important thing we do every day to collect information. It is a skill, it is perishable, it should be practiced and modified when necessary.

REFERENCES

Ajzen, I. (1977). Information processing approaches to interpersonal attractions. In N. L. Collins & L. C. Miller, (1994). Self-disclosure and liking: A meta-analytic review. *Psychological Bulletin, 116,* 457–475.

Al-Simadi, F. A. (2000). Detection of deceptive behavior: A cross-cultural test. *Social Behavior and Personality, 28,* 455–451.

American Psychiatric Association. (1994). *Diagnostic and statistical manual of mental disorders* (4th Ed.). Washington, D.C.: American Psychiatric Association.

Aristotle. (350 BC/1996). *Rhetoric* (W. R. Roberts Trans.). [CD-ROM] World Library (4th Ed.). Irvine, CA.

Aronson, E. (1969). The theory of cognitive dissonance: A current perspective. In L. Berkowitz (Vol. Ed.), *Advances in experimental psychology,* Vol. 4. (pp. 1–34). New York: Academic Press.

Asch, S. E. (1946). Forming impressions of personality. *Journal of Abnormal and Social Psychology, 41,* 303–314.

Aubuchon, N. (1997). *The anatomy of persuasion.* New York: American Management Association.

Berry, D. S., & Landry, J. C. (1997). Facial Maturity and daily social interaction. *Journal of Personality and Social Psychology, 72,* 570–580.

Bigelow, J. (1916). *The autobiography of Benjamin Franklin.* New York: G. P. Putnam's Sons.

Bonhoeffer, D. (1965). What is meant by "telling the truth"? In M. L. Knapp, & M. E. Comadena (1977). Telling it like it isn't: A review of theory and research on deceptive communications, *Human Communications Research 5,* 270–282.

Bradley, M. T., & Rettinger, J. (1992). Awareness of crime-related information and the guilty knowledge test. *Journal of Applied Psychology 77,* 55–59.

Bruck, M. (1999). The suggestibility of children's memory. *Annual Review of Psychology.* Retrieved November 22, 2002 from http://www.findarticles.com/cf_0/m0961/1999_Annual/ 54442306/print.jhtml.

Bucqueroux, B., & Carter, S. (1999). Interviewing victims. *The Quill, 87,* 19–21.

Byrne, D. (1969). Attitudes and Attraction. In L. Berkowitz (Vol. Ed.), *Advances in Experimental Psychology, Vol. 4.* (pp. 35-90). New York: Academic Press.

Canter, D., & Alison, L. (Eds.). (1999). *Offender profiling series: Vol. 1. Interviewing and deception.* Dartmouth, England: Ashgate.

Cassell, P. G., & Hayman, B. S. (1996). Police interrogation in the 1990s: An empirical study of the effects of Miranda. *UCLA Law Review, 43*, 839–931.

Cecarec, J. M., & Marke, S. (1968). Maning av psykogena behov med frageformularsteknik [Measuring psychogenic needs by questionnaire]. Stockholm, Sweden: Skandinaviska Testforlaget. In W. F. Chaplin, J. B. Phillips, J. D. Brown, N. R. Claton, & J. L. Stein (2000). Handshaking, gender personality and first impressions. *Journal of Personality and Social Psychology, 79*, 110–117.

Chaplin, W. F., Phillips, J. B., Brown, J. D., Claton, N. R., & Stein, J. L. (2000). Handshaking, gender personality and first impressions. *Journal of Personality and Social Psychology, 79*, 110–117.

Chandler, M. J., & Afifi, J. (1996). On making a virtue out of telling lies. *Social Research, 63*, 731–762.

Cialdini, R. B. (1993). *Influence: The psychology of persuasion.* New York: William Morrow.

Clark, M. S., Mills, J. R., & Corcoran, D. M. (1989). Keeping track of needs and inputs of friends and strangers. *Personality and Social Psychology Bulletin, 15*, 533–542.

Collins, N. L., & Miller, L. C. (1994). Self-disclosure and liking: A meta-analytic review. *Psychological Bulletin, 116*, 457–475.

Curtis, R. C., & Miller, K. (1986). Believing another likes or dislikes you: Behavior making the beliefs come true. *Journal of Personality and Social Psychology, 51*, 284–290.

Dalto, C. A., Ajzen, I., & Kaplan, K. J. (1979). Self-disclosure and attraction: Effects of intimacy and desirability of beliefs and attitudes. *Journal of Research in Personality, 13*, 127–138.

Davis, J. D., & Sloan, M. L. (1974). The basis of interviewee matching and interviewer self-disclosure. *British Journal of Social and Clinical Psychology, 13*, 359–367.

De Becker, G. (1997). *The gift of fear.* New York: Dell.

DePaulo, B. M. (1992). Nonverbal behavior and self-presentation. *Psychological Bulletin, 111*, 203–243.

DePaulo, B. M. (1994). Spotting Lies: Can humans learn to do better? *Current Directions in Psychological Science, 3*, 83–86.

DePaulo, B. M., Stone, J. I, & Lassiter, G D. (1985). Deceiving and detecting deceit. In B. R. Schlenker (Ed.). *The self and social life.* New York: McGraw-Hill.

DePaulo, B. M., Charlton, K., Cooper, H., Lindsay, J. J., & Muhlenbruck, L. (1997). The accuracy-confidence correlation in the detection of deception. *Personality & Social Psychology Review, 14*, 346–357.

Diagnostic and statistical manual of mental disorders: DSM IV. (4th Ed.). (1997). Washington, D.C.: American Psychological Association.

Dimitrius, J., & Mazzarella, M. (1999). *Reading people: How to understand people and predict their behavior–anytime, anyplace.* New York: Ballantine.

Dimitrius, J., & Mazzarella, M. (2000). *Put your best foot forward.* New York: Scribner.

Dulaney, E. F. (1982). Changes in language behavior as a function of veracity. *Human Communication Research, 9*, 75–82.

Duncan, B. L. (1976). Differential social perception and attribution of intergroup violence: Testing the lower limits of stereotypoping of Blacks. *Journal of Personality and Social Psychology, 34,* 590–598.

Dunning, D., & Stern, L. B. (1994). Distinguishing accurate from inaccurate eyewitness identifications via inquiries about decision processes. *Journal of Personality and Social Psychology, 67,* 818–835.

Edwards, D., & Potter, J. (1993). Language and causation: A discursive action model of description and attribution. *Psychological Review,* 100, 23–41.

Efran, M. G. (1974). The effect of physical appearance on the judgment of guilt, interpersonal attraction and severity of recommended punishment in simulated jury task, *Journal of Research in Personality 8,* 45–54.

Egan, G. (1975). *The skilled helper.* Monterey, CA: Brooks/Cole.

Ekman, P., & Friesen, W. V. (1975). *Unmasking the face: A guide to recognizing emotions from facial clues.* Englewood Cliffs, NJ: Prentice Hall.

Ekman, P., Freisen, W. V., & Scherer, K. (1979). Body movement and voice pitch in deceptive interaction, *Semiotica, 16,* 23–27.

Ekman, P., Freisen, W. V., & O'Sullivan, V. (1988). Smiles when lying. *Journal of Personality and Social Psychology, 54,* 414–420.

Ekman, P., & O'Sullivan, M. (1991). Who can catch a liar? *American Psychologist, 46,* 913–920.

Ekman, P. (1992). *Telling lies: Clues to deceit in the marketplace, politics, and marriage.* New York: W. W. Norton.

Ekman, P. (1996). Why don't we catch liars? *Social Research, 63,* 801–817.

Elliott, G. C. (1979). Some effects of deception and level of self-monitoring on planning and reacting to self-presentation. *Journal of Personal Social Psychology, 37,* 282–292.

Ennis, C. (2000). Listening to children. *Law and Order, 48,* 131–134.

Festinger, L. (1957). *A theory of cognitive dissonance.* Oxford, England: Peterson Row.

Feingold, A. (1992). Good-looking people are not what we think. *Psychological Bulletin, 111,* 304–341.

Fiedler, K., & Walka, I. (1993). Training lie detectors to use nonverbal cues instead of global heuristics. *Human Communication Resources, 20,* 199–223.

Flemons, D. (1998). *Writing between the lines: Composition in the Social Sciences.* New York: W. W. Norton.

Ford, C. V. (1996). *Lies! lies!, lies!: The psychology of deceit.* Washington, D.C.: American Psychiatric Press, Inc.

Freud, S. (1905). *Fragments of an analysis of a case of hysteria: Collected papers Vol. 3.* New York: Basic Books.

Gilovich, T., Savitsky, K., & Medvec, V. H. (1998). The illusion of transparency: Biased assessments of others' ability to read one's emotional states. *Journal of Personality and Social Psychology, 75,* 332–346.

Givens, D. G. (2000). *The Nonverbal Dictionary of Gestures, Signs & Body Language Cues.* Spokane, WA: Center for Nonverbal Studies. On line at (http://members.aol.com/nonverbal2/ diction1.htm).

Gold, J. A., Ryckman, R. M., & Mosley, N. R. (1984). Romantic mood induction and attraction to a dissimilar other: Is love blind? *Personality and Social Psychology Bulletin, 10,* 358–368.

Goleman, D. (1997). *Emotional intelligence.* New York: Bantam Books.

Gosling, S. D., & Ko, J. S., Mannarelli, T., & Morris, M. E. (2002). A room with a cue: Personality judgments based on offices and bedrooms. *Journal of Personality and Social Psychology, 82,* 379–398.

Granhag, R. A., & Stromwall, L. A. (2000). The effects of preconceptions on deception detection and new answers to why lie-catchers often fail. *Psychology, Crime, & Law, 6,* 197–218.

Granhag, R. A., & Stromwall, L. A. (2001). Deception detection: Interrogators' decoding of consecutive statements. *The Journal of Psychology, 135,* 603–620.

Gregory, D. (1999) Conversations of Joe Navarro with Special Agent Doug Gregory, Federal Bureau of Investigation, Washington, D.C.

Griffin, E., & Sparks, G. G. (1990). Friends forever: A longitudinal exploration of intimacy in same-sex friends and platonic pairs. *Journal of Social and Personal Relationships, 7,* 29–46.

Gudjonsson, G. H. (1995). The effects of interrogative pressure on strategic coping. *Psychology, Crime & Law, 14,* 309–318.

Gunlicks, L. F. (1993). *The Machiavellian manager's handbook for success.* Washington, D.C.: Liberty.

Hall, Edward T. (1966). *The hidden dimension.* Garden City, NY: Doubleday.

Hicks, S. (2000). Leadership through storytelling. *Training and Development, 54,* 63–64.

Hare, R. D. (1993). *Without conscience: The disturbing world of the psychopaths among us.* New York: Pocket Books.

Hirsch, A. R., & Wolf, C. J. (2001). Practical methods for detecting mendacity: A case study. *The Journal of the American Academy of Psychiatry and the Law, 29,* 438–444.

Hock, R. R. (1999). *Forty studies that changed psychology.* Upper Saddle River, NJ: Prentice Hall.

Hunt, G. L., & Price, J. B. (2002). Building rapport with the client. *The Internal Auditor, 59,* 20–21.

Inbau, F. E., Reid, J. E., & Buckley, J. P. (1986). *Criminal interrogation and confessions (3rd ed.).* Baltimore: Williams & Wilkins.

Inbau, F. E. (1999). Police interrogation: A practical necessity: *The Journal of Criminal Law & Criminology, 89,* 1403–1412.

Jones, E. E., & Archer, R. L. (1976). Are there special effects of personalistic self-disclosure? *Journal of Experimental Social Psychology, 12,* 180–193.

Kashy, D. A., & DePaulo, B. M. (1996). Who Lies? *Journal of Personality of Social Psychology, 70,* 1037–1051.

Kassin, S. M. (1997). The psychology of confession evidence. *American Psychologist, 52,* 221–233.

Kellerman J., Lewis, J., & Laird, J. D. (1989). Looking and loving: The effects of mutual gaze on feelings of romantic love. *Journal of Research in Personality, 23,* 145–161.

Kleinke, C. L., & Kahn, M. L. (1980). Perceptions of self-disclosures: Effects of sex and physical attractiveness. *Journal of Personality, 48,* 190–205.

Kleinke, C. L. (1986). Gaze and eye contact: A research review. *Psychological Review, 100*, 78–100.

Kleinke, C. L., Peterson, T. R., & Rutledge, T. R. (1998). Effects of self-generated facial expressions on mood. *Journal of Personality and Social Psychology, 74*, 272–279.

Knapp, M. L., & Hall J. A. (1997). *Nonverbal Communication in Human Interaction (4th. ed.).* New York: Harcourt Brace College Publishers.

Knapp, M. L., & Comadena, M. E. (1997). Telling it like it isn't: A review of theory and research on deceptive communications, *Human Communications Research 5*, 270–282.

Kraut, R. E. (1978). Verbal and nonverbal cues in the perception of lying. *Journal of Personal Social Psychology, 36*, 380–391.

Kunda, A., & Thagard, P. (1996). Forming impressions from stereotypes, traits, and behaviors: A parallel-constraint-satisfaction theory. *Psychological Review, 103*, 284–308.

Lassiter, G. D., Shaw, R. D., Briggs, M. A., & Scanlan, C. R. (1992). The potential for bias in videotapes confessions. *Journal of Applied Social Psychology, 22*, 1838–1851.

Leo, R. A. (1996). Miranda's revenge: Police interrogations as a confidence game. *Law and Society Review, 30*, 259–288.

Lewis, D. (1995). *The secret language of success: Using body language to get what you want.* New York: Galahad Books.

Lieberman, D. J. (1998). *Never be lied to again: How to get the truth in 5 minutes or less in any conversation or situation.* New York: St. Martin's Press.

Lieberman, D. J. (2000). *Get anyone to do anything and never feel powerless again.* New York: St. Martin's Press.

Lowndes, L. (1999). *Talking the winner's way: 92 little tricks for big success in business and personal relationships.* New York: MJF Books.

Mann, S., Vrij, A., & Bull, R. (2002). Suspects, lies, and videotape: An analysis of authentic high-stake liars. *Law and Human Behavior, 26*, 365–376.

McGregor, I., & Holmes, J. G. (1999). How storytelling shapes memory and impressions of relationship events over time. *Journal of Personality and Social Psychology, 76*, 403–419.

Meloy, J. R. (1988). *The psychopathic mind: Origins, dynamics, and treatment.* Northvale, NJ: Jason Aronson.

Meloy, J. R., & Mohandie, K. (2002). Interviewing the violent true believer. Behavioral Analysis Program, Counterintelligence Division, Federal Bureau of Investigation, Washington, D.C.

Michelini, R. L., & Sodgrass, S. R. (1980). Defendant characteristics and juridic decisions. *Journal of Research in Personality, 14*, 340–350.

Mitchell, R. W. (1996). The psychology of human deception. *Social Research, 63*, 819–861.

Molloy, J. T. (1975). *Dress for success.* New York: Warner Books.

Morris, D. (1985). *Body watching.* New York: Crown.

Mueser, K. T., Grau, D. W., Sussman, S., & Rosen, A. J. (1984). You're only as pretty as you feel: Facial expression as a determinant of physical attractiveness. *Journal of Personality and Social Psychology, 46*, 469–478.

Navarro, J. (2002). Interacting with Arabs and Muslims. *FBI Law Enforcement Bulletin*, 71, 20–23.

Navarro, J. (April, 2000). Nonverbal communications for law enforcement officers. A series of lectures presented at the University of Tampa, Tampa, Florida.

Navarro, J., & Schafer J. R. (2001). Detecting deception. *FBI Law Enforcement Bulletin*, 70, 9–13.

Navarro, J., & Schafer J. R. (2003). Universal principles of criminal behavior. *FBI Law Enforcement Bulletin*, 72, 22–24.

Nierenberg, G. I., & Calero, H. H. (1971). *How to read a person like a book*. New York: Pocket Books.

Nydell, M. K. (1996). *Understanding Arabs: a guide for Westerners*. Yarmouth, Maine: Intercultural Press.

O'Connor, J., & Seymour, J. (1995). *Introducing neurolinguistic programming: psychological skills for understanding and influencing people*. London: Thornson.

Park, B., & Flink, C. (1989). A social relations analysis of agreement in liking judgments. *Journal of Personality and Social Psychology, 56*, 506–518.

Pease, A. (1984). *Signals: How to use body language for power, success, and love*. New York: Bantam Books.

Porter, S., Campbell, M. A., Stapelton, J., & Brit, A. R. (2002). The influence of judge, target and stimulus characteristics on the accuracy of detecting deception. *Canadian Journal of Behavioral Science, 34*, 172–184.

Rabon, D. (1992). *Interviewing and interrogation*. Durham, NC: Carolina Academic Press.

Rabon, D. (1994). *Investigative discourse analysis*. Durham, NC: Carolina Academic Press.

Rathus, S. A. (1994). *Essentials of psychology (4th ed.)*. New York: Harcourt Brace College Publishers.

Rhodewalt, F., & Davidson, J. (1983). Reactance and the coronary-prone behavior pattern: The role of self–attribution in response to reduced behavioral freedom. *Journal of Personality and Social Psychology, 44*.

Rogers, C. R. (1961). *On becoming a person*. Boston: Houghton Mifflin.

Rudacille, W. C. (1994). *Identifying lies in disguise*. Dubuque, IA: Kendall/Hunt.

Sagar, H. A., & Schofield, J. W. (1980). Racial and behavioral cues in Black and White children's perceptions of ambiguously aggressive acts. *Journal of Personality and Social Psychology, 39*, 590–598.

Sapir, A. (1996). *Scientific Content Analysis (SCAN)*. Phoenix, AZ: Laboratory of Scientific Interrogation.

Saral, T. B. (1972). Cross-cultural generality of communication via facial expressions. *Comparative Studies, 3*, 473–486.

Sarason, I. G., Sarason, B. R., Pierce, Shearin, E. N., & Sayers, M. H. (1991). A social learning approach to increasing blood donations. *Journal of Applied Social Psychology, 21*.

Schafer, J. R., & MacIlwaine, B. D. (1992). Investigating child sexual abuse in the American Indian community. *The American Indian Quarterly, 16*, 157–167.

Schafer, J. R. (2002). Making ethical decisions. *FBI Law Enforcement Bulletin, 71*, 14–18.

Stewart, J, E. (1980). Defendant's attractiveness as a factor in the outcome of criminal trails: An observational study. *Journal of Applied Social Psychology, 10*, 348–361.

Strom, J. C., & Buck, R. W. (1979). Staring and the participant's sex: Physiological and subjective reactions. *Personality and Social Psychology Bulletin, 5*, 114–117.

Strum, B. W. (2000). The "storylistening" trance experience. *Journal of American Folklore, 113*, 287–304.

Szczesny, P. (2002). Subject interviews. *Law & Order, 50*, 126–128.

Vessel, D. (1998). Conducting successful interrogations. *FBI Law Enforcement Bulletin, 67*, 1–6.

Vonk, R. (2002). Self-serving interpretations of flattery: Why ingratiation works. *Journal of Personality and Social Psychology, 82*, 515–526.

Vrij, A., Dragt, A., & Koppelaar, L. (1992). Interviews with ethnic interviewees: Nonverbal communication errors in impression formation. *Journal of Community & Applied Social Psychology*, 199–208.

Vrij, A. (1993). Credibility judgments of detectives: The impact of nonverbal behavior, social skills, and physical characteristics on impression formation. *Journal of Social Psychology, 5*, 601–610.

Vrij, A. & Winkel, F. (1993). Objective and subjective indicators of deception. *Issues in Criminological & Legal Psychology, 20*, 51–57.

Vrij, A. (1995). Behavior correlates of deception in a simulated police interview. *The Journal of Psychology, 129*, 15–28.

Vrij, A. (1996). Misverstanden tussen politie en verdachten in een gesimuleerd politie-verhoor. [Misunderstandings between police officers and suspects in a simulated police interview]. *Nederlands Tijdschrift voor de Psychologie en haar Grensgebieden, 51*, 135–144.

Vrij, A. (1997a). Individual differences between liars and the ability to detect lies. *Expert Evidence, 5*, 144–148.

Vrij, A. (1997b). Wearing black clothes: The impact of offenders' and suspects' clothing on impression formation. *Applied Cognitive Psychology, 11*, 47–53.

Vrij, A., Edward K., Roberts, K. P., & Bull, R. (2000). Detecting deception via analysis of verbal and nonverbal behavior. *Journal of Nonverbal Behavior 24*, 239–263.

Vrij, A. (2001). Detecting the liars. *Psychologist Special Issue: After the facts: Forensic Special Issue, 14*, 11, 596–598.

Vrij, A., Edward, K., & Bull, R. (2001). Police officers' ability to detect deceit: The benefit of indirect detection measures. *Legal & Criminological Psychology, 6*, 185–196.

Vrij, A., Edward, K., & Bull, R. (2001). Stereotypical verbal and nonverbal responses while deceiving others. *Personality & Social Psychology Bulletin, 27*, 899–909.

Wainwright, G. R. (1993). *Teach yourself body language.* London: Hodder Headlines Plc.

Walters, S. B. (2000). *The truth about lying.* Naperville, IL: Sourcebooks.

White, W. S. (2001). Miranda's (Miranda v. Arizona, 86 S. Ct. 1602)) failure to restrain pernicious interrogation practices. *Michigan Law Review, 99*, 1211–1247.

Winkel, F., & Vrij, A. (1990). Interaction and impression formation in a corss-cultur-al dyad: Frequency and meaning of culturally determined gaze behaviour in a police interview setting. *Social Behaviour, 5,* 335–350.

Zunin, L., & Zunin, N. (1972). *Contact–The first four minutes.* New York: Ballantine Books.

INDEX

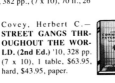